I Held Hands with the Devil

A SURVIVOR'S STORY OF ABUSE, RESILIENCE, AND REDEMPTION

MARY LONG

QUILL
HAWK
PUBLISHING

QUILL HAWK PUBLISHING

Cover designed by Ava Wood, Fins and Feathers Designs

ISBN: 978-1-965142-57-8 (Paperback)
ISBN: 978-1-965142-58-5 (Hardback)
LCCN: 2025912321

Trigger warning: Sexual abuse content

For my children Max, Cash, and Fallon. May you never stop dreaming of doing better in this world.

Contents

Introduction

Healing can come in many forms. Sometimes it may come from simple growth, while other times it may require intense therapy or various medications. The effectiveness of the treatment depends on the nature of the trauma and the individual's response to it. Despite what medical books say, the journey of healing and recovery is deeply personal and driven by the individual's mental processes and ability to transition. This is a story of my healing journey, shaped by the trauma that ultimately led to who I am today.

I will guide you through the earliest childhood memories and very expressive experiences, with the hope that my story can help others who have experienced similar trauma and situations find a way to grow from their trauma and find peace within their present-day life.

CHAPTER ONE

The Hardship of Cancer

I remember that day very clearly. Sitting in that cold room as the people hustle and bustle about. Having left arm pain creates panic in the medical field. I thought it might be her heart. But what did I know, barely twenty years old, with this new friendship my mom and I had bolstered together. She looked so frail in that hospital bed. Maybe it was the fear on her face, maybe it was the fear she saw on my face, but we both knew something was amiss. Then they brought it in. The image that changed our lives. Slid up into the faint light to shine upon us like a dreadful dark cloud.

It was the size of a football. I was young, but I could make it out, and it didn't belong on any X-ray. The tone of the room hushed. The looks on everyone's face as they stared at what could only be death hanging in our midst. That day changed my life. Maybe the change wasn't initially what I thought. Sure, a cancer diagnosis throws a wrench in anyone's life plans. But ultimately, it had shown me how precious life was and how little time we are actually given. At that moment, it just meant Mom had cancer.

CHAPTER TWO

Memory of a Forgotten Child

I was a little girl with crazy blonde hair; I had one rambunctious older brother and one who was darn close to being my twin. We were inseparable. Maybe it was the fact that we were so close in age. Maybe it was a part of the fact that we were the only thing that was stable in each other's lives. One thing for sure, if you separated me from my brothers, I cried.

Daycare probably hated us. Couldn't leave the little blonde girl in her room. She screamed for her brothers the entire time. Oh, only if they knew. Only if they understood that James was my protector, my safe haven. Without him, I felt lost. So being in a room away from my brothers felt like being on a deserted island with no escape.

I have an impeccable memory. One that many people would love to have. I mean, how many people can say that they remember their first birthday? I do! I had a Raggedy Ann cake.

My mom carried me into a room filled with people. My brothers perched beside the blazing candles with eager anticipation on their faces, awaiting to taste the sugary goodness. Then they turned off the lights. Why did they turn off the lights during kids' birthdays back then? I began to cry, and everyone began to sing.

I was a year old when my dad left my mom. My mom claims she kicked him out because he did not come to my first birthday. I remember them fighting that last day they were together. We had a blue and yellow parakeet. There was mold dripping down the wall, probably from a leak in the ceiling.

My Aunt Lois was there and shooed the boys into the backyard so they would not be around the fighting. I wanted to go too, but the grass was taller than I was. My aunt scooped me up in her arms and proceeded to walk me around the block. I remember a movie theater sign with an Indian chief out front. When I told my mom and aunt about the memory years later, they were quite freaked out by the detail because it was spot on. I was so young. What a crazy, wonderful, cursed memory that I have. I have been told that you remember things in your life better when they are attached to trauma. Interesting considering how much I remember about my childhood. Not all memories were bad, but it feels as though a lot of bad things happened. The bad seemed to outweigh the good.

Another early memory was when I could barely walk. My mom had moved into an apartment with a man after she and my dad divorced. He had a lot of plants. They were stacked on a shelf in the kitchen. The shelf was located on the floor, providing easy access for little hands. My toddler self knocked a plant off the lower shelf. That man became very upset. Not long after, another plant was on the ground. I remember that he picked me up, held me up high, and started shaking me violently. I know he was screaming but it was the height that scared me.

My mom came around the corner and told him it was not I who had knocked over the second plant, but her. He put me down, and I toddled into my brother's room. There were James and Philip, their faces frozen in fear. I crawled beside James for protection. There we sat, the three amigos in an empty room with just a deflated beach ball, scared to death. I never saw that man again after that day. But this sparked our journey together, leading us into a spiral of hell. A nice woman named Wanda watched us from time to time. She was kind and gentle and I loved her. Philip cried a lot for Mom while we were with her. She lived in a small house, and we slept in the living room on pallets on the floor. She bought us each a toy to keep us occupied.

I picked out a Fisher-Price record player. I loved being able to place each record on the turntable and listen to the melody play on the plastic records. Philip had picked out a Coca-Cola truck, complete with miniature bottles that fit into a sleeve to be loaded onto the truck. James, with his high-intensity personality, chose a big truck. He was obsessed with crash up derby, and he played it well. He used his big truck to smash Philip's truck into pieces.

Our time with her when I was close to two years old was brief. We spent time bouncing between our mom's and our Aunt Linda's house after we left Wanda's house. Aunt Linda had a lot of kids. When Mom took us to her house, I remember them arguing because Aunt Linda knew Mom would disappear after dropping us off. My Mom would lie next to us until we fell asleep. This always made me afraid, as I knew that when I woke up, my mom would no longer be there.

We were two and three years old at the time. We must have been some very stressed-out kids because Philip and I woke up with poop in our pants at that time. Maybe it was Aunt Linda's prompting, as she was tired of taking care of us while our mom was out doing who knows what, but my mom finally obtained a trailer for us to live in.

It wasn't much, but we were happy. It had two bedrooms, and most of the time, my brothers and I slept together on the same mattress on the floor. When it was cold, we slept in my mom's bed, under an electric blanket, since we rarely had heat.

I remember my mom not being there a lot. Just James, Philip, and I running around playing. We had toys but hardly any food. One morning, she woke up late. Too late for day care—I'm sure those day care workers were happy that we didn't show up that day. But that meant no breakfast for Philip and me, as James was at school.

We were hungry, and when Mom opened the cabinet door in the kitchen, there was only a can of pork and beans. Philip began to cry; he hated beans. I was excited because I loved them. It wasn't unusual to only have beans or cereal without milk. I also remember eating Vienna sausages a lot. They are quite disgusting, but when you are hungry, you'll eat just about anything to fill your belly.

When we were very little, I think I was younger than three years old, we got up early to watch cartoons. A man walked out of my mom's room and started questioning whose kids we were. She told him that they were her kids. She could tell the man was not pleased, and she started taking her anger out on us by yelling.

There were soda cans all over the living room. She insisted that we start drinking them as she thought we had gotten them out while she was asleep. We started to drink them, but then we began to cry. They had old cigarette butts placed in them, but she didn't believe us that something was wrong with the drinks, and she screamed even louder.

The man became angry with her, and he began to yell at her because they had been drinking the drinks the night before. He left, and I never saw him again. I'm sure that was right before we were dropped off at Aunt Linda's house, since we were cramping her style of being single. That was when my mom's personality began to change significantly. At least it was when I remember it changing. She began to yell at us more. Being a kid and running around having fun seemed to irritate her. I do not remember being spanked, but I am sure that I was.

My Aunt Lois told me later that she stayed with us during this time. I do not remember her being there. I mainly remember being alone with my brothers. I also remember a man, maybe someone my mom was dating at the time, was at our trailer house. I had climbed onto the arm of the couch to sit on it like it was a horse. My mom became angry and started yelling. The man quieted her and said I was being a kid. He knelt in front of me and spoke to me softly. My tears stopped, and I remember feeling happy. Kindness goes a long way.

We came home one day to the trailer house, and all our things were packed in boxes. I had several purses that I loved, which were on top of the boxes, and I wanted to grab them and take them with me. My mom told us we were not allowed to take any of our things from the boxes.

My past had shown me that when boxes were involved, you never saw those items again. I did not want to lose my purses. Later, I found out my mom had been dating the landlord, and I guess his time with her was over. We were being evicted. We were sent back to Aunt Linda's.

It wasn't all roses at Aunt Linda's house. Her husband yelled a lot, and frankly, he was quite dumb. It was also one of the only times I remembered someone other than my grandpa touching me sexually. My oldest boy cousin had his fair share of me, but my older girl cousin told him to stop because I was too young.

Yes, kids molest kids. No, it is not experimenting. It is traumatized kids who do not know what's normal and what's not normal. They proceed to do to others what has been done to them. I am grateful for that girl cousin to this day.

I don't know how long we stayed at Aunt Linda's that time. Some things had changed. My mom's hair fell off one day. It scared me to death. Her head was almost bald with small sprigs of blonde hair sticking up from her scalp. I realized later that she was wearing a wig. She claimed this was why she couldn't take care of us. She told everyone that she had brain cancer.

Word got around, and my dad found out that we were living at Aunt Linda's and my mom had cancer; he got us from Aunt Linda's. He took us to his smoke-filled apartment. We had toys, and most of all, we had my big sister, Gena.

Gena was like a mom. She loved us. She fed us and took care of us. I never wanted her to leave. We stayed together for a while. I remember my dad being there because I remember him smoking, but he was gone a lot with work.

Then we all moved. We were always moving. Suddenly, I had a new mom. She became my dad's third wife, and she gave me a little brother. That little brother was my treasure. Maybe that is where my love for babies came from. She was good to me and my brothers. I know we lived there long enough to watch Bobby, my little brother, grow into a toddler, but it was not long enough.

I had a phobia of water. I am not sure when it started, but I only remember hating bath time. My mom had little patience with my fear, and usually, I had water dumped on my head as she tried to wash me quickly.

Nothing seemed to help ease my fear. It was not until a little old lady named Mary entered my life. She was frail and thin. She had black hair that was probably dyed black. Her son lived with her, and his room was decorated with snakes, and I hated napping in his room. I thought the snake might come alive and bite me.

She was nice to both Philip and me. Sometimes, she watched Bobby as well. One day, I must have smelled bad, because she decided I needed a bath. She filled the tub with around 2 inches of water. I screamed the whole time until she put me in the bath and leaned all the way over the side and held me as she laid me back in the water. She took a cup and gently poured water over my head and washed my hair, keeping the water from getting on my face. It was the first time I remember not being scared. I look back and appreciate someone taking the time to be gentle and reassure me that I would be ok.

Not long after, I found myself nestling in another woman's lap. One I lovingly called "Piggy" because I could not say her name correctly at the age of three. She became my dad's fourth wife. "Piggy" had a daughter, and I thoroughly enjoyed having a girl to play with. We also started seeing our mom at times. My mom was with another man, once again. This man did not like kids, so it was not long before he moved on. Our lives with Piggy were enveloped by years that resulted in a new trauma for my brothers and me. She gave us a new little sister and, with her, another side of Piggy.

Who could blame her? There she was, with a new baby, three additional kids—one that was uncontrollable—and her daughter in a tiny house. The house had one bedroom, and it didn't have a door. It was like a modern-day dining room. She had no escape from all the hysteria of raising those wild children. Her mental status broke.

I remember her having a fit of rage and throwing Play-Doh cans at us and locking James in the bathroom for hours. Then the beatings began. The shame started. We longed for our mom. She would visit, and we would visit her, but Mom did not save us. That was also the time when we started visiting Grandpa.

One time when Mom picked us up, she took us to her apartment. She placed a record on the record player, and we danced to "The Name Game." We were excited because we thought that this meant she would keep us, yet again, disappointed. She claimed that this new place was Aunt Lois's house and that our aunt did not like kids, so we were not allowed to live there. She drove us back to our dad's house, and we sadly walked back into our darkness of shame and rejection.

I cannot imagine living in the '70s with no skill set and having to try to make ends meet. Kids are expensive, and my mom could not afford to feed us. Our aunt had a child, and she gave him up for adoption. My mom told me stories, and later my aunt told me stories about the cousin and how he was adopted. To this day, I still do not know the whole story involving the cousin. I only knew Aunt Lois had him until he was eighteen months old and then gave him away.

Considering how Aunt Lois always told me that she hated children, up until I was around thirty-six years old, I believed my mom when she said that Aunt Lois hated kids, which is why we could not live with her, and that she gave her child away because she did not want to be a mom This also makes me wonder if my Aunt Lois had a hand in my mom leaving us so much.

One time at grandpa's house, I was very hungry. I was young, maybe six years old. As my mom poured a bowl of cereal for me, I watched roaches crawling into the box. I complained, as I could see them floating in my goat's milk. She became angry at me and told me to eat around them. She had no care for me, no care for illness or my safety.

Bed-Wetting

I know this was a problem from a very early age. Most people would chalk it up to being potty-trained too early. Maybe it was that my bladder was not growing as fast as my body? Maybe it was psychological? I know that as a child, it was only one thing: shame. I woke up almost every morning in a wet bed. My mattress reeked of urine.

I'm sure I was the stinky girl at school. The hardest part of all was sleep-overs. When I was in first grade, a sweet girl invited me to have a sleepover. My mom warned me that if they found out that I had "accidents," I would not be allowed over anymore. Excited, I decided to try to stay the night. I had a plan. I would not drink anything before bed, and I would pee before bed.

We had so much fun. Her mom had a wide variety of musical instruments and knew how to play each one. She had a piano, and I was fixated on it. I wanted to play desperately. She had a playhouse that her dad had built, which resembled a small house on the inside. When it was time for bed, her mom pulled out a real bed and I snuggled in.

I woke up wet. I had failed. I tried to smell the mattress, but it didn't smell like urine to me. I prayed that they would not find out. I wanted to be invited back. I liked my new friend.

The next time I saw her at school, she was kind. She told me that maybe it was too early for sleepovers and that her mom was not mad, but we needed to wait until I was older. I will never forget that kindness. She did not shame me; she gave me empathy.

My older sisters Debbie and Gena had another little sister who was three months younger than I was. So confusing, I know. This sister was kin to them through their mother. My older sisters and I shared a dad. I look back on it now, and it all seems so odd. Debbie's mom would allow me to stay the night with the sister.

Her bedroom was white with beautiful white furniture. Her closet had shelves lined with an array of Barbies and Barbie accessories. I always wanted to play with them, but the little sister never wanted to play with them. I am sure that to her, they were boring. To me, they were a little bit of heaven.

I was jealous of their other little sister when I was growing up. She had her mom and dad together. She lived in a house. She had a bed and lots of toys. She also had the curliest, prettiest hair. I was a scrawny little blonde girl whose hair was never combed. I'm not sure how her mom put up with me, but she never spanked me or made me feel bad, even when I wet the bed.

I was ten years old before I agreed to a real sleepover again. It was with April, and she became one of my best friends growing up. It helped to have friends who did not shame me when I was trying to heal from things I did not talk about.

Potty Training

I'm a stubborn adult; I am sure I was a stubborn child. But one thing is for sure: when most kids wet the bed or their pants, they are not doing it on purpose. The punishment for a four- to five-year-old when I was growing up was to wear your soiled underwear on your head while your stepmom went into town. Because of actions like this, I felt shame; it was my friend.

For my brothers, it meant a beating to their private parts. To this day, I do not know if my stepmom or my real mom left the bruises on their penises; I remember them being there. If I were beaten, I have somehow blocked it out. Most of the time, I remember James jumping in front of the paddle or belt and taking my spankings for me.

Seeking Attention

I remember that I thrived around anyone who would give me attention. I consumed compliments, hugs, and especially gifts. I dreamt of being a princess in a big fluffy dress or Dolly Parton sitting on her swing and singing. I would watch her on TV before kindergarten when I was at Wanda's house. Dolly Parton was kind and beautiful, everything a five-year-old wanted to be.

If I heard that I was someone's favorite, I reveled in it. I yearned for acceptance and love. I'm not sure if that's normal. But I can tell you, evil people prey on this. They take advantage of this void. They groom you slowly with sweet words. How pretty your hair is, or how sweet you are. They say, "You are my favorite," just to watch big, bright, brown eyes beam with joy.

Being the favorite is not always a good thing. When you say, "Stop" or "No," they manipulate you even more. "Don't you love me?" And the best line: "Do not tell anyone or I'll get into trouble." It was not until years or decades later that I understood what that meant.

Another female family member had told the school about the sexual abuse she had endured when she was younger. They must have gotten into trouble; unfortunately, it only made them sneakier. See, evil cannot be corrected. Correction and discipline only help them devise a more deceitful way so as not to be caught. Evil must be exposed. Only then can it be stopped.

Bridge Creek

We lived close to Blanchard, Oklahoma, for my first through third-grade years. It was way out in the country. Our acreage was just dirt. We stayed in a nice trailer house. We had food, we had clothes, but most of the time, I went to school dirty, my hair not completely brushed, with a nice rat's nest in the back of it. This was the product of fine, blonde hair and a mother who was not patient with me.

We made friends in our little area. Some were nice, some came from more toxic situations than we had endured. Most of us had lice. I guess it was a common thing in country schools. I had lice, so bad; they were falling out of my hair. One time while sitting in the gym waiting for PE to start, a lice fell off my hair and landed on my eyelashes. That bug was strong and held my top and bottom eyelashes together. I had to pull hard to get it to release.

When we moved to Blanchard, we had just moved from our dad's back to our mom's. My hair was long, down to my butt. I would have to pull it to the side to sit on the toilet. My stepmom had grown it out and took good care of it when we lived with our dad. She also brushed it nicely and made sure it was clean.

My mom, after a while, cut it off at the shoulders. The boys had their hair buzzed. I guess this was her treatment for lice. I remember the neighbors had gasoline poured over their heads to get rid of their lice. Probably a good thing my mom cut my hair instead of introducing toxic chemicals next to our brains.

James struggled in school. He was also mischievous. He lied on his eye exam because he wanted glasses. They were thick and ugly. I remember my mom and stepdad being so angry. I look back now and laugh. He was probably hard to raise. Philip and I did well in school, but watching James have issues caused me to have anxiety that I may not pass my grade. That lasted until fifth grade.

I was afraid of having bugs in my hair, ticks especially. In second grade, on the school bus, I felt a tick on the back of my head. I danced around like a Junebug was on me until a boy plucked the tick off my head and saved me from my panic attack.

I am not sure how long it took, but I developed a fever. My mom had to pick me up from school because I was very sick. To my understanding, I had been in bed for several days with a high fever. I do not remember eating, drinking, or using the bathroom. I guess letting your child die was not on my mom's list that year, so I was taken to the doctor.

I sat on the exam table, lethargic. The doctor asked my mom all kinds of questions. Then he asked about ticks. I piped up and answered, "Yes." The look on my mom's face! She was shocked. The doctor combed through my hair and found an embedded tick head in my scalp. He diagnosed me with Rocky Mountain spotted fever and sent me home with several antibiotics. I think my mom was more embarrassed than anything. If she had just run her fingers through my hair, or perhaps if she had washed my hair for me? She might have found the cause.

I missed a lot of school because it took me a long time to recover. But this wasn't when our lives in this household started to fall apart; it started soon after. My stepdad was heading into town. Philip asked if he could go with him. Only one child was allowed to go, as he was taking his small truck. The older kind with a stick shift in the middle and air conditioner knobs that stuck out far. It was technically a three-seater, but a very tight three-seater. Philip was little, like me, but the stepdad did not want to take the two of us.

Not long after they left, my mom got a phone call. My stepdad and Philip had been in a bad car accident, and they were unsure if Philip was alive. My mom was frantic. James and I piled into the back of her car, and she sped away. I was crying, thinking that I had lost my best friend. Who would play stuffed animals with me? How was I going to live without my best friend?

We pulled up to the truck. They had been in a head-on collision with a large car. A teenager was driving under the influence of alcohol and crashed into my stepdad's truck at a fast speed. We were not allowed to get out of Mom's car. So, we had to sit there watching the police and the firemen until my mom returned.

We drove that night to Southwest Medical Center, where Philip had been sent. He needed surgery on his brain. He had sustained a brain injury.

When my stepdad saw the car coming, he told Philip to get onto the floorboard. He thought it would protect him. This action was what caused him to sustain his injury. The impact of the other car caused Philip to fly forward, and the air conditioner knob jabbed into the right side of his frontal lobe. My stepdad, thinking Philip was dead, walked to a nearby house to call for help. He was bloody himself, as he had collided with the windshield.

As told from the woman in the house's point of view, she heard a knock on her door. When she opened her door, she saw Philip standing there. His forehead was crushed on one side and open. She wrapped a towel around his head. She said she thought about rinsing his head under the sink. The doctor said that if she had done this, he would have died.

He spent hours in surgery, having bone fragments removed from his brain. He was away from home for most of his third-grade school year. I did have to grieve the loss of my brother, as he was not the same when he returned home.

He would no longer play with me. He found me annoying, and he was embarrassed about the scar on his forehead. With this added stress, things in Blanchard began to tumble downhill. It was only a year before we were uprooted again. This time, we moved back to the city for more poverty, hunger, and stress.

I drove back to the land in 2014; the acreage was overgrown with trees and greenery. A new trailer in place of the old. Memories that had eluded me flooded back like waves. Such as flying kites so high that we could barely see them in the sky. Playing kickball in the dirt with the other children in the neighborhood. Picking carrots out of our garden. I began missing the closeness my brothers and I shared back then. I pray my children never lose their sibling bond.

Intelligence versus Common Sense

Chris has often said to me that I am so smart, that I am dumb. It is hurtful to hear, and I would rather say, I'm ditzy. Sometimes, I do not get jokes; it takes me a minute. Other times, I'm so literal, I miss what is happening altogether. This is what amazes me about my childhood. I was intelligent. At least, I was book smart.

When I was in first grade, I developed a slight stutter, which significantly exacerbated my shyness. The thought of having to read out loud frightened me. I could not read ahead because I had not developed reading comprehension skills yet. So, every time I had to read a paragraph and talk about it. I had to reread it multiple times to understand what I had read.

To make things worse, when people gave me verbal instructions, sometimes it felt like I was hearing a foreign language. I would have to have them repeat it over and over until I understood.

As I grew older, if I was left to myself, I could fly through schoolwork if I did not have to read out loud. I was often scolded for working ahead of the rest of the class. Mrs. Woods, my first-grade teacher, must have seen my potential. She encouraged me every chance she could. She taught me how to sit like a lady. How to wait my turn.

One of the most inspiring memories I have of her was when she allowed me to read to the class. Not just any book—books I had written and drawn the night before. During most of my first-grade year, she allowed me to do this. The shy, dirty, unkept little girl whom she saw potential in.

In fifth grade, it was my first year at Lexington, and we had to take the standardized state testing. I somehow scored high enough in reading to be placed in the gifted and talented program in my sixth-grade year. It stated that I scored an average of college-level reading in the fifth grade. Still shocked myself, but if left to my own, I can read and comprehend quite quickly, especially as I got older.

Young Coping Mechanisms

As a small child, I often daydreamed. I couldn't pay attention while the teacher was teaching. Zoning out, daydreaming, whatever you want to call it, it got me into trouble more often than not.

I was intelligent, but I did not pay attention in class. I now realize that I am a hands-on learner, and if I have to sit and listen for long periods, I tend to zone out. I don't sit still for very long. Perhaps I have some form of undiagnosed ADHD. It does not matter; what matters is that I recognized my coping mechanisms.

Zoning out is also used by children in abusive situations to disassociate themselves from the present, not to feel any emotion. I used it to fend off boredom a lot, too. My imagination was incredible when I was younger. If I daydreamed, it was like being in a book. I was being a princess, flying in the air, or going on a great adventure in my head.

After going through pretty intense therapy and schooling, I now know that daydreaming like mine was trauma-related. It was my coping mechanism for being in fight or flight mode for so long.

This is why people who are having a psychotic break may appear catatonic. They are lost in the daydream, so to speak. Their bodies have nothing left to fight the demons. We all need rest. Rest is good. Daydreaming and zoning out are a type of rest. It is this rest that my mind needed during some of the hardest times in my life as a child.

I wish I hadn't been scolded in school for daydreaming; I wish I had someone who took me aside, with my stinky clothes and lice, and tried to find out what was going on in my little life. I was brushed aside as "not my problem." Children do not deserve this. They deserve love, attention, and sympathy. They deserve to be noticed, cared for, and to be children.

Switching schools frequently did not help with my daydreaming, nor did it improve my learning process. Math was exceptionally hard for me. When I entered fourth grade, other kids were already mastering their times tables, and I felt thoroughly confused. My handwriting was worse than that of any doctor that I have met in my life.

I eventually learned my times tables. My handwriting improved after I met Donna Thomas. As her handwriting was beautiful, I desired to have beautiful handwriting like hers.

In high school, algebra came easily, and I would often tutor others in Mrs. Cummings' class, as she was quite slow when teaching. My favorite teacher in school was Mrs. Johnson, whom we respectfully called Mrs. J. She encouraged me to pursue a career in journalism. She said I had a gift for storytelling. It sounded boring. The human body fascinated me, and I was dead set on the medical field.

One of my coping mechanisms now is planning. I like to plan trips, vacations, anything that will leave a good memory. I love being spontaneous and doing fun things during the day or night, but when it comes to a big decision that will have a significant impact on my life, the decision needs to be made thoughtfully. It must be thought through, contemplated, rationalized, with my options weighed, and then decided on for many days, weeks, or months before a decision is made. I do not do well with fast changes. Anything that happens too quickly can throw me into a state of numbness. This is my coping mechanism to keep me from being hurt. Then I may overthink the situation for hours, days, or weeks until I conclude that everything will be ok.

Nun

Looking back, I really don't know how many stepfathers I had. There were many, and most were horrible. At one point in my life, starting in first grade, life was pleasant. This is when we lived in Blanchard.

I rarely saw my grandpa. Maybe it was because we lived far away from him. Maybe it was because my mom married a man who came from money. Either way, I soaked up the goodness. This stepdad had a mom with my name. She was a dance instructor who taught me dance and baton. One good thing that she taught me was that people who truly love you do not require anything from you. If someone requires something from you, they are not genuine.

She loved me; I felt loved. I never wanted to leave her side. Her son was a good role model for my brothers. He coached their baseball team and took them to the Boy Scouts. He cheered at James' football games, and he scratched my back.

Our house was pleasant, and it felt safe. We had food at every meal. We had nice clothes and warm beds to sleep in. We also started going to church. I do not remember going before he came along.

At the age of seven, we attended a large church. A man dressed in fine clothes and fancy shoes preached the good word. There was an altar call. I knew that I was supposed to go down to the altar. I looked at my mom and told her to go. She declined, my stepdad declined, but I couldn't. It was as though a rope was pulling my heart; I was being led to salvation.

I made my way out of the pew to the altar like someone was offering free dolls, toys, or candy. Or maybe that is what adults felt when they win the lottery, or how people feel when they are on The Price Is Right? I know one thing: I was called to get a prize, and I was going for it.

I knelt in the aisle as the altar was filled. I stretched out my arms forward and gave up my life to Him, Jesus. There I knelt, in what we now call a child's pose, ready for the Lord to use me.

At one point, I sat up and looked behind me; on either side were my mom and stepdad. Maybe they felt that they had to go with me. I will never know, but they were there. Later that day, I saw a nun on TV and felt that God called me to be a nun. I was to live my life wholeheartedly for the Lord.

Looking back now, I have to laugh: If God wanted me to be a nun, I ruined that in my teen years. Ultimately, I decided that being a nun was not for me. I wanted to be a mom, and being a nun would get in the way of those big plans. I was a whole seven-and-a-half years old when I decided against it.

Wanda and Tommy

I know I have elaborated a little on Wanda and Tommy. Two people who did not have to take in two extra kids but graciously did. Their neat little stone house nestled in the depths of the poverty-stricken area called the Stockyards. It was like living in a mansion in that part of town.

They placed a bunk bed and a single twin in their second bedroom, making us all feel at home. We were tucked in every night, with clean sheets and a kiss. I was made to sleep without my undies to "let things air out." And I had no fear of the night; it was for health reasons, not for easy access.

We woke up every morning to a breakfast of eggs and milk. I was not fond of either. It's funny now knowing that milk was the reason for my severe diarrhea because I was lactose intolerant. We were never in want. Our clothes were new, and our shoes fit well. We were made to dress properly, so I played in the dirt with my cancan dresses, frilly socks, and patent shoes.

There was one TV in the living room, located on the floor. It was the perfect spot for little eyes to sit so close that you felt like you were at the movies. We did not have a care in the world. We only knew love. I was held on a lap that did not desire more from me. I was taken to school and picked up. I napped when I needed to. I was healthy—both mentally and physically.

I loved watching Dolly Parton and The Muppet Show. One time, I asked Wanda why Miss Piggy's nose was so big. She said it was because she picked it too much when she was a kid. Scared me to death. I was afraid my nose was going to be that big if I picked my nose.

I finished my kindergarten year living with them. Every day after school, we loaded into the back of the pickup truck and went to the small store down the road. We were allowed to get one snack. My statistical little mind thought one snack needed to last a long time, so I went for the large package of Chips Ahoy! cookies. My brothers chose a small candy or a candy bar. It wasn't long before James complained that I had more snacks than he did, and I wasn't allowed to do that anymore.

Wanda bought me my first tricycle, and I made friends with a sweet girl who lived behind the house. Her name was Tina. She was a beautiful redheaded girl who lived with her grandmother. Her grandmother was mean. Tina was spanked often.

Although I was allowed to play at her house, she was not allowed to touch her toys until the appointed times during the day. I happened to touch a dollhouse when I was visiting her house one day, and I was told to leave. I could hear Tina screaming from her whooping while I was walking back to Wanda and Tommy's.

I also learned how to roller-skate while we lived with them. There was a church down the road that let the neighborhood kids roller-skate in their gym. Two teenage girls helped me skate. They were nice.

Several years later, both of those girls became my cousins when my mom married their uncle. It was a strange turn of events, but it solidifies that I do not believe in coincidence, and everything happens for a reason.

I have never forgotten the kindness of a woman and her husband who did not have to be kind. They gave me a love that made me feel like I was their child and provided me with the security that allowed me to be one. They gave me memories that gave my heart warm feelings.

I drive by where the house used to be and reminisce sometimes. Seeing the memories dance around the yard as our childhood played out before us. The time we spent with them was short-lived; we lived with them for approximately six to eight months. They are both long gone from this world, but their impact was truly great.

CHAPTER THREE

The Root of All Evil

Grandpa

Money makes people do awful things. Things they may not do otherwise. Evil people know when others can be bought with money. Evil people know who they can manipulate. It's almost as though the demon in them tells them who to prey on as well.

When I am in a crowd, I can tell you who is a bad person. My radar is strong. I was told once that it was my demons that recognized the demons in others. I'm not sure how accurate this is, but I can assume it's correct.

The times that my mother took us for a "visit" to Grandpa's, we always went to a small, dark house. It smelled of cigarette smoke and dog urine. The walls were tainted yellow from the smoke that hung heavily in each room. There were newspapers under the kitchen table, and the carpet was sticky from the multiple accidents their chihuahuas had. Roaches crawled on the countertops and sometimes on the walls.

My mom would drop us off for babysitting. It was more like we were watching ourselves. We played in the dirt driveway, ran around the backyard, and "smoked" grass rolled in paper bags, pretending they were joints.

He had an old boat that didn't have a motor, and we would use the garden hose to bring back the color on the faded hull, pretending that we were painting it. There was an old delivery truck that we played in, and a small barn where he kept his goat. Lots of things for kids to climb on and jump from.

Then one day, at Grandpa's, while the boys were out back, the Devil made his move. My innocence was stolen. I saw the Devil in my grandpa that day. It was brief for him, as the boys bombarded through the side door. The interruption from my brothers threw a kink in his chain. It did not stop him.

After that, He found ways to distract the boys. One time, he sent them into the grocery store to buy ice cream and made me stay in the truck with him so he could fondle my private parts. I was more upset about not getting to go inside. I did not understand at the time the horror he was inflicting on me.

Money

My thoughts about being served up for money to my grandpa came from what history held. My mom seemed to love money more than she loved her children. It was not long before I was dropped off alone. Too young to remember why, but I have my suspicions. I'm thankful that I was such a tiny young girl. I cannot imagine what pervasive thoughts he had about his acts upon me if I were older or even bigger boned.

My loving, protective older brother appeared quite different from Philip and me. We were blonde with big brown eyes. James had brown hair and big blue eyes. We were tiny, and James was quite large. He protected us, yet picked on us all the same. He would tease me that I was Miss Piggy off The Muppet Show because my mom would say that my nose was turned up like a pig's nose. He teased Philip that he had a conehead. We had no idea it was a classic premature head my brother toted around all those years.

My teasing stopped the day I had enough. I was digging in the dirt with a hand shovel when I was four years old. We were at Wanda's house. James was on the front porch, and he called me "Miss Piggy" for the very last time. I pulled back my little arm and let that shovel fly. It smacked him right in the face, cutting his eyebrow. Wanda was good to me about the whole situation. I picked my switch from the nearby tree and took my whooping, and James never teased me again.

When James was eight, he came back home from Wanda's, different. He was withdrawn. He pushed us away. It wasn't until years later that I found out how his world fell apart.

See, my mom kept having miscarriages. Through a family friend, she learned about a lady who was about to give birth and needed a place for her baby. That lady was Wanda. That wonderful woman, whom I only remember love coming from, had a bleak story. She had been married and found herself pregnant with her fifth child. Her husband was not kind to her and accused her of adultery. Back then, that was a bad omen for a family. Her father hid her away while she was pregnant, and she had a nervous breakdown during the pregnancy.

She did the best she could for the baby. On a day in April 1970, she went into a Texas hospital as Joyce Stidham, my mom, and had a baby. His birth certificate reads as though my mother gave birth to him. The awful grandpa named him and became the oldest son.

Wanda was always close by. She reminds me of Moses' mom. She made sure that he had a home, but kept an eye on him until the time was right for the truth to come out.

Five thousand dollars was all it took. I cannot imagine how much money that was in the late 1970s. For five thousand dollars, our mom permitted Wanda to tell James that she was his biological mother. She gave up her rights, she disrupted our lives, and she destroyed his life for five thousand dollars. At this point, I am not sure who was in the wrong. Maybe Wanda thought that she could love the hurt out of him, but time proved different.

I am not going to lie, I was jealous. From that point on, I was convinced I had been adopted. I was not close to my mother, always choosing every other woman over her. Sadly, I was not adopted. I know I am different. God created me different than others in my mom's family. To this day, I have encouraged all adoptive parents to be as honest as possible with their children. I never want another child to face the deceit that my brother experienced. I can still see the hurt on his face if I close my eyes long enough.

That takes me back to my memory. Call it photographic, call it a curse, but I remember things. Things that I love, things that make me want to gouge my eyes out, things that no child should experience. This desire for money is what led me to believe that I was being taken to my grandpas for money. I seemed to have been dropped off when his wife had doctors' appointments, or she had to see the elderly neighbor. More often than not, I was left alone with the devil.

Sasha

As I lay in bed snuggling with the cutest half-schnauzer/half-wired-haired terrier mutt, named Sassy, right now, I remember growing up with cats. We rarely had dogs, except Cajun when I was older, and the precious miniature schnauzers that we were given when we were young teens. I often wondered why we did not have more dogs than we did. Was it the dog hair? The excessive barking? Was my mother just not a dog person?

When I was around ten or eleven years old, my aunt gave my brother and me miniature schnauzers. My brother's was a boy and mine was a girl. I named her Sasha. She was so cute and tiny, and I loved her dearly. One day, we came home from school, and Philip's dog was gone. Mom said he had died of parvo (canine parvovirus) while we were at school. I believed her. Who wouldn't trust their mom? The following day, Sasha was gone. Mom walked me to a spot between two trees where she was buried. I used to talk to that spot. I buried my hamster there several years later.

Now I look back, lying in my bed, petting Sassy, my current dog, and knowing I really could not trust my mom. I believe my stepdad either killed the puppies, because he loved to shoot stray dogs, or my mom sold them for money since they were registered. This is another story that illustrates how growing up with a money-hungry mother in the 1980s was truly hurtful.

Clothes

It is funny how things influence your entire life. I cannot wear cute off-the-shoulder dresses, not even when I wasn't chubby. You see, a child does not know right from wrong until they become aware of it. They only know what attracts good attention, bad attention, or attention in general. Many times, I was laid beside my grandpa, who was "lying down to sleep." I was told to take a nap with Grandpa.

Innocently, I agreed. Lying there with my tiny self, in tiny clothes. He struggled to pull my pants down. He wouldn't keep his hands away from my private parts. He was frustrated that my jeans were too tight. To please him, I promptly jumped up and ran to the only bathroom in the house, his house. I changed out of those jeans and into a dress for easier access for him. A child will comply to please an adult. It is NOT consent.

I walked out of that bathroom, proud. I remember standing in the doorway of the bathroom, pulling the shoulders of that dress down to expose my shoulders. After all, that is what I saw my mom and Aunt Lois do to please men. I proceeded to go back to Grandpa's bedroom and get back into bed with him. I was five years old.

Evil is smart. It is cunning. He knew my act would bring attention. He rolled away from me as I crawled into bed, and I said, "Now it'll be easier, Grandpa." Not long after, my mom and Aunt Lois popped their heads into the doorway of the room. I do not remember what they said. I just said, "I'm more comfortable now." Then I fell asleep fast. Whether that evil man persisted after I fell asleep, I may never know. I slept so deeply as a child that I would wet the bed often.

The part that disgusts me the most is how both women KNEW what he was like and still allowed me and encouraged me to be in that bed with him. Later that day, I was asked by both of them if Grandpa had touched me wrong. With his words bouncing in my head, "Don't tell anyone or I'll get into trouble," I promptly lied and ran outside to play. I lied often. I cannot lie now; you can read it on my face. And no off-the-shoulder dresses for me.

We could not afford nice clothes for most of my life. I was fine with hand-me-downs and clothes that didn't fit well. At the age of ten, I wore a size six in girls' shirts. Such a tiny thing, and thankful that I didn't grow fast, as clothes may have been even more sparse.

At the age of twelve, my other aunt bought me the most beautiful sweater for my birthday. Birthdays are another story. I rarely received birthday gifts. This birthday, I felt so special. I cherished this sweater, wearing it to school proudly. I finally felt beautiful in what I was wearing. It did not last long. Since we lived in the country and used well water, most of the white items we washed turned yellow from sediment in our well. My beautiful sweater became a dingy yellow color.

I felt mad at my mom; I thought that she had washed it at home to get back at me, to hurt me. I do not understand the need for a mother to feel in competition with their daughter or to sabotage their daughter's happiness.

At the age of thirteen, Cristina's parents, my friend who lived walking distance from my house in Lexington, gave me an outfit for my birthday. It was when stirrup pants were in style. It came with a matching shirt. I finally had a complete outfit that was in style and matched. I wore those leggings out. I was very thankful that they thought of me.

Around this age, I was also attending a church in Purcell. I had joined the choir and was heavily involved in it. One day, an elder asked me to come outside, as there was someone who wanted to meet me. Out in the parking lot was an older couple, the woman had black hair that looked like it had been dyed. They were both much older than my parents. They were driving a pickup truck.

They introduced themselves as the Wadleys. They were kind and asked if they could adopt me. I was taken aback. Was it my shabby clothes, my unkept hair? Was it that I looked like an orphan, or was it the potential in me that made them feel that they could foster growth? I politely said, "I do not think my mother would like that." When I went home and told my mom about the encounter, she made me quit going to church.

CHAPTER FOUR

Everything a Teenager Never Wanted

Growing Up in Lexington

When we moved to Lexington, we had a nice, brand-new trailer. Sometimes, I had my own room. Sometimes, I shared with Philip; it depended on whether James lived with us or not. For the first month, we did not have running water. We bathed in the rain. Used the toilet in a makeshift outhouse (hole in the ground). I do not think I brushed my teeth for a whole month.

Thankfully, we had a well installed right before school started. We had the nice trailer for only a year before my stepdad quit his job, and we had no place to live. They sent Philip and me to stay with our dad for the summer.

We spent the summer in Reno, Nevada, and when we returned, a very old 1970s trailer was in the place of the other trailer. It was a small two-bedroom. That second bedroom was only big enough for a twin-sized bunk bed and a small bedside table. My brother and I had to share. James did not come back to live with us after that.

When we first moved to Lexington, I saw a girl who lived down the street. It was probably a fifteen-minute walk. I walked to her house and knocked on the door. A woman answered, and I asked if her daughter could play. I was ten and I was immature, evidently. I did not see anything wrong with that gesture, but it was a source of jokes for years to come from my friends.

Cristina was a year younger than I, but we had so much fun together. She wasn't allowed in her house much. So, we played outside a lot. There was a creek right beside her house, and we could walk in it and come out close to my house. Sometimes I would show up, and she had to do chores before we could play. She had different clothes for playing and school; I just had one set. She also had a little brother and sister. They were twins, and they were babies when we met.

The punishments she dealt with were strict. I didn't quite understand them, as my mom would rather I be out of her sight than punished in a room around her. One summer, I chose to stay over. She was grounded for not eating the crust from her sandwich. She was made to eat sandwiches for breakfast, lunch, and dinner the following day as her punishment. Since I was staying over, it was my punishment too.

She spent a lot of time at our house. Philip, Cristina, and I played together whenever we could. Then a boy moved in next door to us. His name was Chris, and he quickly became friends with Philip. They spent time fishing or shooting guns together. He hardly played with Cristina and me after that.

I hated indoor work. I didn't want to cook or do dishes. I wanted to be outside, clearing the land or mowing the lawn. It was fun. I didn't like my stepdad, but I would rather have been active and out in the fresh air than be trapped inside cleaning. I never learned to cook, but I did learn to bake. I loved to bake, and I still do.

It's funny that high school had great home economics classes. I switched high schools so many times, and each time I moved, the home-ec part was sewing. I never took a cooking class. Probably why I do not cook very often today. I can cook; I just choose not to.

When we finally started school in Lexington. I was in the fifth grade. A sweet girl named Theresa Sherman befriended me. I had the ability to attract hooligans; it took over, and I soon became friends with April and Trulie.

April was tough and she always wanted to fight other girls. She had the cutest stepbrothers, and she accepted me. Trulie was loud, funny, and everybody knew her and loved her. She was the extrovert who adopted this introvert. We became very close, very quickly.

Soon, I was at Trulie's house all the time, staying the night, playing in the creek, or running through the fields. My favorite was calling her horses from the field and riding the horses in the pastures with her cousin DeeAnn. She always let me ride Sugar, a female paint horse.

One time when we were thirteen years old, Trulie and I were riding Sugar bareback. I was in front, and Trulie was behind me. I was wearing stirrup pants, and we were barefoot. She had her feet in the stirrups of my pants. A coat was hanging on a tree, swaying in the wind. It startled Sugar, and she jumped sideways. We both fell off with such force, landing on our sides. It hurt, but we laughed so hard.

Trulie had a big family, and they all lived very close to each other in the country. You could walk to each other's house through the fields or down the street. They would have big get-togethers, and they always invited me. It felt awkward to be around such a large family. Mainly because my mom never took us around our own family. I was not sure how to act in such a large crowd.

Her mom and dad were good to me. Her mom showed me how to cook certain foods we did not eat at our house. I still don't like fried okra; it's gross. She always allowed me to eat the chocolate chips out of her freezer or drink her Hershey's chocolate straight out of the bottle. Maybe she knew that these were things I was not afforded. I do not know. I just know that she was good to me.

As we grew, our mischievous side did too. I lived with Trulie's family several times in my late teenage years. At age seventeen, we went cruising on Main Street in Purcell. I became separated from Trulie and drank way too much alcohol. When we finally joined back together, I couldn't stand up. Trulie carried me up her long gravel driveway and shoved me through her bedroom window. Trulie was 5'2" and I was around 5'5" at that time. I have to say, she was strong. Her driveway was straight uphill.

When she came through her kitchen door, her parents asked where I was. She covered for me and said I had come home earlier with a stomachache. Needless to say, I was given chicken noodle soup the next day by her mom. That was tough to stomach with a massive hangover.

Trulie was a source of strength. We had great times, and we had tough times. I was in a self-destructive pattern, and I hurt her feelings often. We lost touch at age twenty-six, and I'm sure it was mainly my fault. I tried rekindling the friendship many times. The last was in 2010, right around her thirty-sixth birthday.

We went out together and had such a great time. It is funny how time does not squander the love you have for someone. No matter how different our lives were, we still felt close. She died six months later. She was riding with a drunk driver, and he passed a cop while he was going over ninety miles per hour. Frantic, he lost control of his truck. He drove in a culvert doing ninety, and he flipped his truck; everyone was thrown from the vehicle except for the driver. All five passengers were killed.

The police officer saw it all happen in his rearview mirror. He turned around and called the dispatcher for help. He found Trulie; he was a friend from high school, and he had to find her that way. The driver walked away with a slap on the wrist from the judge. A piece of me died that day. I had known her longer than I had known my mother.

Never A Doctor in Sight

When I was ten, my mom married my stepdad, Charlie—the one who moved us to Lexington. This man was loud and loud scared me. Loud meant that you were doing something wrong, and punishment was sure to follow, especially since I was raised in an era when children were expected to be seen and not heard. He never spanked us; he just used emotional torture.

He used small jabs to make us feel stupid: "You have the common sense that God gave to a goat." "What, were you born in a barn?" "Don't you think?" Using these cutting words, over and over until you felt worthless.

However, we did have food on our plates, for once. Our clothes were shabby, and our shoes barely fit, but this was normal. I ran around barefoot for so long as a child that when I did get a pair of shoes, I wanted the laces really tight so my feet wouldn't slide around in them. I walked barefoot a lot, even to stores or on outings.

His aura was negative and scary. We learned to stay away from him. When we walked down the long gravel driveway after the school bus dropped us off, we would look for the end of his eighteen-wheeler sticking out of the end of our driveway. If we saw it, Philip and I would go to our friends' houses instead of going home. Sometimes we stayed the weekend with our friends to escape from how mean he was to us. That dreaded, deep sinking feeling when we saw him home, I will never forget it.

I spent most of my teenage years in Lexington. I made great friends. We spent our summers playing in the creek, catching crawdads, or going fishing. In the winter, we prayed for snow so we could build snow forts. One winter, it snowed so deep that it came up to my thigh; I remember this because I had a cast on my leg from my ankle to my hip.

When I was thirteen, I was on my lunch break at school. We were playing around on a big grassy field. I did a cartwheel and kicked back into the splits. I had taught myself all kinds of gymnastics moves since we could not afford classes. This time, I had landed wrong. When my right leg landed behind me, it knocked my kneecap to the right of my leg. It was a type of pain I had never felt. I rolled to my side, grabbed my leg, and screamed.

A coach came over and told me to get up. I said that I couldn't. He went to get my big brother James. He was old enough to drive and had a truck at school that Wanda had given him. James scooped me up and took me home. It was a ten-mile drive from school to home. Every bump of the ride made the pain radiate. At this point, I was in shock from the pain and trying to pass out. That was December 11, 1987. I did not go back to school for the rest of that semester.

At home, I was met with "you're faking," as the pain only intensified. I was only given Tylenol—no offer for a doctor, no sympathy. I used to have a picture of my hand next to my knee. My knee was the size of a watermelon. How can anyone tell a child that they are faking when their knee is the size of a watermelon?

My mom had rented crutches the following day from the local pharmacy so I could get around in our trailer house. I do not remember how long I suffered before my mom produced Tylenol #3s for my pain. She had them after my grandpa had died that year. They were lifesavers. Considering my stepdad took away my crutches several days after the injury and told me to walk, I needed pain management.

I learned how to get to the bathroom by keeping my right leg bent and going heel-toe on my left foot down the hallway of our small trailer house. Hopping hurt; every thrust downward was like a knife being jabbed into my knee. I slept on the living room floor as I couldn't move well without intense pain. One night after the pain medication had kicked in, I was finally sleeping when my muscles spasmed and my leg jerked. This was probably when my kneecap popped back into place. The pain was intense when this happened.

Around December 20th, my stepdad took away my pain medicine as he had said, "I was getting addicted." I was finally sleeping in my room on the bottom bunk. Trulie was sleeping over, and I woke up with so much pain. I could not wake her up by calling her name; all I could grab was my huge history book, which I grabbed and threw onto the top bunk. It woke her up. She retrieved some pain medicine, and I was able to get back to sleep.

I weaned myself off the pain medication but was still unable to put pressure on my right leg. It was December 24th, and I was going to visit my older sister Debbie because my dad was coming into town. As soon as he entered my sister's apartment, I begged him to take me to the hospital. Several hours later, I was told I broke the head of my femur and fitted into my leg-length cast.

The next day, I showed up at my mom's house. I wanted to show those people how they had let me down. They let me lie around for two solid weeks with a broken leg. Their faces said it all; my stepdad dropped his head, and my mom looked shocked. All she could whisper was a small, "I'm sorry." It took several days before I could put pressure on my knee. I learned how to walk in that cast and even run a bit. It looked very funny, but I did not care. I was so happy to be mobile again.

The worst part was that I had a cast for eight weeks. Once my cast was off, I realized my thigh muscles had atrophied. I was prescribed physical therapy and given a brace for my knee. Physical therapy wasn't possible. We couldn't afford a doctor's visit or a dentist's visit, much less a visit to physical therapy.

I rehabbed my knee and thigh muscles myself, a fourteen-year-old learning to strengthen her own quad and hamstring muscles while also strengthening the tendons to hold her kneecap in place. It took six months before I could walk on my own without the brace. One more thing to chalk up to "what I would never let my kids go through."

Arkansas

My first real memory of Arkansas dates to the age of ten. I'm not sure if our dad had intended to drop us off at our aunts and uncles, or if it was just something that happened. Maybe we begged to stay with them?

I had cousins my age. The oldest girl was two years older than I, and her little sister was three months older than I. They were more mature than I was in some ways, but more redneck in others. They knew how to do laundry and other things kids their age shouldn't know but spoke like they lacked intelligence.

I do not remember being hungry while we stayed with them. Looking back, maybe we were just used to hunger. It was fun and wild, with no parental supervision most of the time. Her mom had horses, which seemed to be deemed more important than her actual children. I never understood this situation.

The house was dilapidated. Their car was on its last leg, but they had horses that were well fed. It was my first time riding a horse. I learned how to place a saddle and bridle. I learned how to go with the movement of the horse when it ran. It was a magical feeling.

We also did crazy stuff, like eating fruit out in the pasture. I am not sure what we ate! I remember my cousin called it a sweet and sour. It resembled a pomegranate. We drank from streams and ran barefoot through the fields.

One time, when we were doing our laundry, the oldest girl cousin and I were heading out to hang our clothes on the clothesline when she stepped on a nail. Instead of doing what I would do, which was scream and cry and be a big baby, she stomped her foot. Thinking it was just a briar and trying to loosen its grip. This caused the nail to dig deeper into her heel. Once she realized what was causing her pain, she fell to the ground and cried out for her mom. My aunt, a short and round woman with crazy hair and a vocabulary of a ten-year-old, came running out of the house and started barking commands.

We did not have a telephone, and the nearest one was over on the other side of the pasture, through some woods at the neighbor's house. My uncle had taken the car, so we couldn't drive there. Barefoot and without underwear underneath my dress, as we were cleaning the few pairs that we had, I took off running through the woods to the neighbor's house. Scared to death of a bear eating me, I made it to the neighbors, out of breath and needing to pee. They drove me back to the house to find my uncle waiting in the car to take my cousin to the ER. She recovered, and I learned that I could run through the woods barefoot if someone I loved needed it.

Once she had healed, our older boy cousin took us for a joy ride in the car. He was only fourteen years old and already knew how to drive. This was my first experience with any wild driving. We did donuts, and he would drive very fast, then pull the emergency brake to spin the car like the Dukes of Hazzard. I felt scared but exhilarated. My first taste of adrenaline.

He taught me how to drive. Later, he became a stock car racer. I like to joke with my kids the reason I drive fast is because he taught me how to drive. I may have been in a wild situation, but sexually, I was safe.

We spent another time with them at the beginning of the summer of my thirteenth year. It was only around four weeks, but it felt like a lifetime. This house was in worse shape than the one from my tenth year. Cardboard boxes were stapled to the walls for insulation. We rarely had food or running water. But we had fun!

We spent almost every night cruising the main drag in Russellville. My oldest girl cousin taught me how to drive a stick shift, and we snuck out as often as we could. We would go to the lakes and swim. Fishing was fun, and we hiked as well. I had my first kiss from a boy, although it was not something I expected, but I thank him to this day for teaching me how to kiss. Then, I was sent back to Oklahoma after I contracted mono, and the authorities were called. I'm not sure where my aunt and uncle were, but I developed a fever and didn't wake up for several days.

My oldest girl cousin became worried, and we walked to the neighbor's house to use the phone to call her aunt so I could get some medicine. Her aunt picked us up and gave me some aspirin. The fever quickly dissipated. Unfortunately, the neighbors called CPS, and they came the next day.

She told them that her parents were long-haul truck drivers, and since her brother was seventeen years old, they allowed us to stay. When my uncle came back, he called our dad, and my dad came to get me and took me back to our mom.

My brother Philip spent the rest of the summer in Arkansas when I was thirteen. He came home in time for school. One day, an officer called my mom. Philip had been caught stealing fishing equipment while he was in Arkansas. It was very expensive equipment. He was given probation and was not allowed to return to Arkansas for two years.

I remember him crying as Mom told him about the probation. She was comforting him and then turned to me and said, "I expected this out of you, but not him." I was taken aback, shocked by her words, but I do not know why I was shocked. There were multiple occasions when she would tell me that she never wanted a daughter. She only wanted boys, as they were easier to raise.

I was never really into drugs. I honestly was afraid I would be a statistic and die my first time trying them. I had only tried a beer at age fourteen. We stayed out past curfew that night, in Oklahoma. Back in the '80s, in a small town, the sidewalks rolled up at midnight. Four teenage girls, one of whom was driving the car, were pulled over for a muffler that was dragging; this was my only visit to a police station. I only sipped that disgusting beer; it was the curfew that led me on the adventure in the back of a police car.

We all had our moms called, and mine arrived quite pissed. I think she was more embarrassed than anything. She grounded me from going into town for the rest of the summer. It was quite a punishment. At age fourteen, you are coming alive to being popular. I spent that summer stuck at home while others were allowed to go to the public pool or attend fun sleepovers. I'd like to say that I learned my lesson; maybe I did, maybe I didn't. I just know I have never been in the back of a police car again.

Fast forward, I'm sixteen years old, and Philip and I have traveled to Arkansas to visit our dad. My cousins promptly took me to another town to do what Arkansas kids in the late '80s and early '90s did—party, drink, and swim in rivers. This was the year when I learned how alcohol could destroy your life. I was highly intelligent, but with alcohol, I had a low IQ.

New people meant new adventures. I tried marijuana for the first time. It is crazy how your circle shifts once alcohol and drugs enter your life. My desire for clean-cut boys faded to the jaded-tattooed type. I'm pretty sure that this was when I started allowing the title of "preyed-upon, naive, easy-to-use" to settle upon me.

I desired love, and I had no idea what love looked like. I allowed that teen boy whom I had met that summer to abuse me emotionally. With each session of partying, any amount of self-esteem I had faded into the background. After the summer ended, I tucked my tail and headed back to Lexington, Oklahoma. He proceeded to play mind games for over a year. Coming to Oklahoma to take me back to Arkansas, promising that I was "the one," just for me to be emotionally abused and for me to leave again.

At one point, my cousins, this boy, his sister, and several others piled into a pickup truck and headed to Ft. Smith, Arkansas. We all thought that we would go there and find great jobs and make it rich. We ended up sharing a hotel room. A week had passed, and no one had found a job. Taking turns stealing lunch meat from the local grocery store, my boyfriend's sister and I set out to find jobs ourselves. The hotel took pity on us and employed me and the sister.

They sent me with the maid and sent the sister to answer the phones. This made sense, as I was homely-looking and the sister was pretty. We made it for a week and had our first paycheck. We both bought large pizzas and ate an entire pizza all by ourselves. Then, after everyone had been fed, we used the rest of our money for gas and drove back to my boyfriend's mom's house.

I want to say I learned my lesson; I did not. But I did learn to tell that boy, "No." I'm not sure how he ended up in life, but he probably wasn't a happy person. Anyone who causes others emotional turmoil is likely an unhappy person.

My cousins all started using harder drugs. I'm glad that I left. I would not have wanted my life to trail down that path of destruction. I will always love my cousins; I pray that they are clean, sober, and happy. They had hard lives. Their parents died horrible deaths when they were older. They were not taught good coping skills, nor were they shown how to be productive adults. They have literally had to wing it their whole lives. I pray that they find peace.

Drugs

Drug issues did not stay in Arkansas. I switched high schools multiple times over the course of four years. One semester at Choctaw, then back to Lexington, followed by a stint in Morrilton, Arkansas, and finally Moore High School, before returning to Lexington. At Moore High School, I met a boy while cruising twelfth street. I was seventeen, my two best friends were pregnant, and I was bored. He introduced me to his friends. They were all younger than me, and I could drive. The saddest part was that the only other girl in this new group of friends was fourteen. I enjoyed her friendship, but she came with toxic baggage: her mom.

I can say that it was one of the only semesters in high school where I barely skipped class. I made straight A's. The young girl's mom was a drug dealer. She would hand us a bag of pot every morning before school. We stayed high every day. One day, while sitting in class, I realized that if I did not leave this group, I would go nowhere in life. After school, I called Norma, Trulie's mom, and asked her if I could move back into her house. She let me and freed me from the demon that was hell-bent on destroying my life: drug addiction.

Marijuana was still around, but not in my face. As we grew older, I watched my friends move from marijuana to crack and then to meth. Some addictions last years, some decades. I thank God every day for the intuition to not stay on that path, for saving me from my self-destruction.

Cigarettes

Everyone I knew smoked. Everywhere I went, smoke was floating in the air. I can't even remember how many times a lit cigarette has burned me. Just to be told, "Watch out, it's your own fault." Oh, how that burn stings!! I spent most of my childhood with a runny nose and a horrible cough. I remember that any time I could, I would stand in front of any window unit air conditioner to let the cold air fill my nostrils and lungs. It felt so refreshing.

My cough kept us from doing many promised things, or at least that's what Mom said. Philip supposedly had asthma, too. I honestly think that it was because she never had the intention of doing anything fun with us, or maybe the man who had promised the outing had backed out.

I have many memories of coughing until I almost passed out, feeling as though I could not take a breath after coughing out my last bit of air out of my lungs. Probably some form of undiagnosed asthma. Luckily, I did not die or suffer brain damage from lack of oxygen. Philip's cough was always worse than mine. He was scrawny. Born prematurely, his lungs were already crappy. That did not stop the smokers. I can remember car rides and no window being rolled down. How did we even breathe?

As we grew, smoking continued. It is no wonder that I hate smoking. It literally disgusts me. Not just the smoke itself but watching someone put a cigarette in their mouth. Even vaping disgusts me.

At the age of eighteen, I went to a doctor on my own. He listened to my lungs and asked how long I had been smoking. I informed him that I was not a smoker. It was years of living with people who smoked in the house and the car.

One time when I was around nineteen or twenty, my little sister Jill and I went to Arkansas to visit our dad. When we walked into his house, there was a smoke wall four feet down from the ceiling. The smoke hung so heavy that it looked like we had walked into a bar.

My dad and his girlfriend smoked in the house with no ventilation. They took us to dinner and smoked in the car, with no windows down. We rolled our windows down in the back seat and hung our heads out of the windows like dogs trying to get some fresh air. That woman died ten years later from lung cancer.

My mom and stepdad smoked in their house, as well. My mom barely smoked her cigarettes. She mainly let it burn in the ashtray while playing a video game on her Nintendo. Their house was not ventilated. My stepdad, when he was home, smoked four packs a day. It was not until after my mom died of lung cancer that he moved the smoking from his chair in the house to the front porch. I think he felt guilty about her death. Watching a loved one die of lung cancer does that to you.

What led to my mom's diagnosis of cancer was this weird shoulder pain that she kept having. She had only achieved her goal of being a hairdresser at the age of forty-four. She was proud, and she was exceptional at it.

Marty, my second husband, joked that she didn't have lung cancer but a hairball from being a hairdresser. He was always funny.

Everyone loved my mom. She was funny, goofy, loved practical jokes, and was a liar. All a facade, everything about her. Her stories were made up; she lived another life in her head. Others did not know this, but I did. I think that is what made me despise her as a child.

This pain was real, though. She wasn't faking it. She rarely complained of pain. She had seen her doctor at least three times in a month to have her left shoulder injected. Knowing what I know now, as a health care provider, this treatment was dangerous. She should not have had steroids that close together. Steroids raise your blood sugar, and cancer feeds on sugar. I finally convinced her to go to the ER, as it could have been her heart. While looking at an X-ray of a football-sized tumor in her left upper lung, it sure felt like the world stood still that day.

Bear or Man

In the spring of 2024, there was a trend on social media over which option a woman would rather run into in the woods: a bear or a man? Most women picked the bear. Your chances of being mauled and killed were about 50/50, but with a man, more than likely it would be a slower and more painful death, as well as the high probability of sexual assault.

My daughter was a couple of months shy of fourteen when she got her first boyfriend. He was a cute little thing with big blue eyes and acted more like a ten-year-old than a fourteen-year-old.

When he looked at her, it was so precious. His eyes beamed with joy. Fast forward three to four months, and he had started putting stipulations on who she could be friends with. With red flags everywhere, I made them break up. I know, mean mom. Don't worry, I let them get back together after I had a firm talk with him. This leads me back to the fact that evil people cannot be corrected; they can only be exposed.

I was several months shy of fifteen years old when I first met Albert—the man who detoured my teenage life. I was at my sister Debbie's, taking care of his nephew. It was a strange family connection, as he was my sister's cousin, but not my cousin. They were related through her mom's side; she and I shared a dad.

He had big blue eyes, dark hair, and dimples. He was eighteen years old. He gave me attention; I was the gangly, skinny, shy girl that no boy at school showed interest in. Here was this older guy acting like I hung the moon. I saw him every weekend when I went to my sister's. Fast forward several months, and I was smitten.

After several months, when we were standing outside my house one night, talking, I looked up at the night sky. It was always so beautiful at night, in the country, in Lexington, Oklahoma. I saw a shooting star, and at that very moment, he asked me to marry him.

It felt like a fairy tale. I said yes, sure, when I'm eighteen, after I graduate. I had plans. My goal was to become a pediatrician. There was no way I could be a housewife. At ten years old, I had made up my mind—I would never depend on a man. I watched my mom jump from man to man, just so we could eat. I watched my stepdad quit jobs on a whim and left us wanting. I was shipped off to my dad for the summer countless times because there was no way they could feed us. Just for him to leave us with relatives most of the time, so that there would not be enough to eat with them, either.

That same night, Albert told my mom that he wanted to marry me. She seemed so excited. She was always good at lying. Probably why I loathe liars to this day. He departed, and I went to sleep on cloud nine, not knowing my near future would become hell on earth.

Several weeks later, it was Christmas Eve. My sister, Debbie, was working on Christmas Eve. I had her two kids who were three and four years old. Albert and I also had his two nephews, who were nine months and five years old.

Albert drove me to my house to get clothes for the night; my stepdad was home. My stepdad was a long-haul truck driver and was only home, maybe one to two days a week. I remember my stepdad telling Albert that he was no longer allowed to see me, as he saw the age difference and knew something was not right. I went numb. Albert convinced my mom and stepdad to let him take me to my older sister's house for the night, as he had four children and needed help taking care of them. He promised my mom and stepdad that he would bring me back in the morning for Christmas.

My sister lived in Moore, and he lived in Nicoma Park—both drives were very far away from Lexington, Oklahoma. It was going to be an even longer drive than usual. As we started down the long, gravel driveway leading away from my house, he turned to me and said that I would never see my mom again. I did not question him. I felt it. It wasn't a statement; it was a threat. I sat quietly in the passenger's seat the whole drive. I did not know what to think. I did not know what to do. I did not know what to say.

The next day, we handed the kids off to their moms, and he drove me to his other sister's house, a place my family could not find me. Scared of him, I kept quiet. He called my mom and told her that if she did not agree to sign marriage papers, she would never see her daughter again. Unsure of how far he would go with his threat, I stayed quiet. I always stayed silent to keep the peace.

A month later, in a courtroom, my tiny self married a monster. My mom was present, and so was his older sister. His sister had taken a pregnancy test in my name, saying that I was pregnant, to allow the courts to proceed with the marriage. I was not pregnant. The ironic thing about this marriage, back in the day when everything was placed on paper, the page number that our license went onto was on page 666—a sign.

I was a fifteen-year-old scared little girl, whom he would not allow to call anyone after we were married. He followed me around the house. He made me quit school for fear I would leave him. He forced sexual relations on me every night, regardless of whether I was sick, tired, or menstruating. If I did try to speak up, he went and grabbed a gun and put it to his head, screaming at me that I was "making him do this" and that I was going to be the reason that he killed himself.

Distraught, I would beg him not to do this, not kill himself. I begged him not to kill me. This would happen two to three times a week for the entire year I was with him. We moved constantly because he refused to work. At fifteen and a half years old, I walked down to Sonic in Nicoma Park and obtained my first job. I was tired of starving, so I became a car hop, which was quite hard as I was extremely shy. A week later, he showed up at my work. He had obtained a job as the manager at the facility to keep an eye on me.

Con artists are cunning. He had no experience of being a manager, but there he was. After much persuasion, I enrolled in high school the following school year, still determined to complete my education. He allowed it, but with consequences. Most days, I was so tired at school from him keeping me up half the night with his mind games or forced sexual activity, that I would sleep in class.

He was also an atheist. He would try to trick me into saying things that proved his atheism was true and my Christianity was not. His torment was never-ending. I would stand firm in my belief that Jesus was in fact real. He is also the Son of God. No matter how hard he tried, he could not shake my faith in Christ.

He would say that he idolized Jerry Lee Lewis. He said that man did it right by marrying a thirteen-year-old. "Get 'em young and raise 'em right" was his motto. He didn't see me as a wife or even a person. I was his possession, and he did to me what he saw fit.

One day, while at work at Sonic, I was making onion rings. It was quiet, and I was focused on my duties. He came up behind me with a knife. He put the knife to my throat and slid it across. My heart dropped; I grabbed my throat as fear welled up inside of me. Thankfully, it was the dull side. Then he said, "See how easy it would be to kill you," and laughed hysterically. Sometimes, he would drive me around Lake Stanley Draper and tell me that he could kill me and bury me out by the lake, and no one would ever find my body. I believed him.

I had made friends with a boy from Sonic, and he would often give me a ride from school to work. He was kind. One day, we walked into Sonic after school together, and Albert was standing behind the counter holding the gun, that dreaded gun I had seen too much of. He pulled the trigger while screaming, "I know you have been cheating on me." Then he laughed that crazy, psychotic laugh. My friend and I stood there in fear. What if he had missed? What if he fires it again? Should we run? He had fired a blank in the gun. My heart did not know the difference. The psychological trauma kept increasing.

On my sixteenth birthday, a year after being kidnapped and sexually assaulted by someone who I can only assume was a sociopath, I wanted something for myself. I wanted my driver's license. He refused. He was afraid that I would leave him. He ran to get the gun and proceeded to play his game. It was at that moment that I wished for death. Deciding that dying was better than this life, I boldly spoke up: "Do it, put me out of my misery." He fell to his knees, crying. I got up, walked over to him, and out of the door to a pay phone (yes, I am that old).

I want to say that it ended that day, but it didn't. I spent two more years avoiding him, watching over my shoulder, all the while still married to him. My spirit was broken, and life had lost its enjoyment. I barely passed my classes in high school, and I was in self-destruct mode. Most of the time at school, I couldn't go to lunch. The secretary would call me out of class and tell me not to leave the building, as he was sitting outside in a car waiting for me. It was a living nightmare. It affected everyone around me.

Then one day, when I was almost nineteen, he called and asked for a divorce. He had met another impressionable girl and wanted to marry her. Poor girl, I wonder how her life really turned out. I was free, but not really. When social media became a thing, he tried reaching out to me. No matter what, I didn't feel free, putting me on high alert until the day he finally pulled the trigger and ended his own life in 2019. Thirty years of making sure a sociopath didn't kill me.

This leads me back to my daughter, I saw my life repeating in her. My sweet girl was fourteen years old, and she was still with her boyfriend. He ran off her three closest friends. She was alone; she only had him.

Later, she made new friends; he tried to run them off. They would only do things together, thus keeping her from being able to do them with her friends, such as going to the fair or out to the movies.

He often went to the movies with our family. She seemed happy and in love. I started noticing in pictures how his smile had faded. As a matter of fact, he rarely smiled at all. They were two years into the relationship, and he was sixteen years old. She was a couple of months away from sixteen. It was September of 2022; she went on a family trip with him and his family.

He was getting high (we didn't know he was getting high, every day). He terrorized her mentally and physically. This was not disclosed to me until after the relationship had ended. I didn't know anything was truly wrong with the relationship until a day in December 2022. The Devil showed up in her boyfriend that day.

What started the events of their relationship demise was when my daughter had her brother's car and was taking her best friend and a teenage girl from our neighborhood home after school. A boy approached her in the school parking lot and offered her gas money if she would take him home. It was very cold outside, and he had no way home, as he had missed the bus. After much prompting from her friends, she did take the boy home. He was a friend of her boyfriend's, but she had anxiety in the car and feared she would get into trouble.

I had come home from work shortly after she arrived home from school, and she was talking on the phone to her boyfriend. She handed the phone to me and said he wanted to talk to me. He was upset, as he thought she did not think about him with her actions when she took the boy home.

I took up for my daughter because I had raised my kids to help others. He would not hear me, and I would not hear him. I handed the phone back to my daughter and said, "Y'all need to work this out yourselves." The look on her face will haunt me forever. She screamed, "I do not want to talk to him, I do not even want to be with him!" It was not anger she was expressing; it was fear.

She grabbed the phone and ran to her room. I sat down for a moment, trying to gather my thoughts. How did I miss it? How did he slip it past me? I had let her down. I went to her room, and she had him on the phone's speaker. He was screaming profanities at my beautiful daughter. I walked over to her, pushed the button, and hung up on him. Frantic, she called him back, afraid of being in more trouble. She put her finger to her lips to tell me to be quiet. He proceeded to cuss her out even more for hanging up on him.

For over twenty minutes, I listened to this young man berate her with insult after insult. My PTSD was full-blown triggered. She was finally able to tell him it was over. His attitude changed drastically. He began to apologize, begging her for another chance. Then the little devil had the nerve to text me. I told him that if I ever heard him talking to her in that manner again, he would never see her again. He had no idea that I knew.

She did take him back that night but thankfully broke up with him the following day. Then she blocked his number. This is when I found out exactly what he had done to her for the past two years. From forcing himself on her, to cutting out her friends, to making her get rid of leggings or tight shirts. He isolated her and tried to control every part of her life. He made her life all about him.

After several weeks away from him, I saw my daughter become brighter in her eyes. She was free. I knew that feeling but hated that she had gone through it. I knew this curse so well. She had stumbled into her own form of hell, and I missed it.

It didn't mirror my hell, and because evil people adapt when someone tries to correct them, he was able to keep it hidden. This is why evil people must be exposed. The friends who were with him in the car while he cursed her recorded his outburst and craziness that he had unleashed on her that day and sent the video to numerous people around school. He left school within the semester.

She still deals with the impact of the torment she went through. She is slowly getting back to herself. She will, at times, still be triggered and start panicking that she will get into trouble for saying hi to someone in the school hallway or smiling at the wrong person. These types of things never really leave you; they just fade into the background noise. They will pop up from time to time in life, and each time, hopefully, you learn to deal with them better and eventually heal.

Albert

I do not recall hearing the word gullible before... him. That sociopath who tormented me for years. It was not unusual for him to tell me a story—and my sweet soul would believe him—just to have him laugh at me. I had only experienced true deceit from my grandpa before him.

One day, while performing my carhop duties at Sonic, he told me that I had been chosen as the National Carhop by Sonic. Unsure how I could have won, I was delighted. The other co-manager took me to his car to listen to a cassette tape that was supposedly mailed to the facility. I think this was the first time I remember someone having remorse for me. He apologized for Albert's evil joke and then proceeded to tell me that I was worth more than I was getting. He said that I needed to rethink my life.

Once back inside Sonic, out came the words, "You're so gullible, you'll believe anything." That sociopath laughed and clapped as though my pain was a circus act for him. It is no wonder that I hate laughing and clapping at the same time now. It is also a big reason I do not trust words. Some people can be so cruel.

Albert was the youngest of three children. He had two older sisters. He lived with his mom, so that meant that he and I lived with his mom most of the time. He rarely worked. If he did have a job, it was only for a couple of weeks or a month, and then he would quit. We moved to Nebraska a couple of months after we were married. He had heard of a pork plant that was hiring and paid exceptionally well.

We had to stay in a motel for several weeks. We lived off macaroni and cheese, as this was all we could afford. I found a free cat in the paper, and I named him Joey. He kept me company while Albert worked.

None of the apartments in Nebraska were affordable. We had to travel thirty minutes away to rent a house. He had made friends with someone who worked at the plant. Together, we rented a house. It was a scary two-story house. We had no furniture. We slept on bed sheets on the ground. I think it lasted several weeks before we packed up and moved back to Oklahoma.

During this time, his mother had moved to the house next door. We were living in her other house. That was when I would walk to Sonic and obtain my first job. I tried to make things normal, or as normal as I thought they could be. Still longing for Trulie, longing to see my brother or other family members, still stuck with just him. Isolation is crazy; once you are isolated, you can be brainwashed more easily.

When I left Albert, he killed my cat, Joey. He tried to tell me that a dog had attacked Joey, but I did not believe him. It was my first experience with how some people take rejection. They will do anything to hurt you back.

CHAPTER FIVE

My Parents

My Mom

I knew nothing more as a child except that my mom was dark-skinned and thin. Her teeth were stained blue from her mom taking tetracycline while she was pregnant with her. She was funny and loved practical jokes. She would dance with her fingers when driving. She loved records, and we danced to The Rocky Horror Picture Show often. People loved her. They adored her. How could they not? She played out to be whatever people wanted her to be. She adapted to every situation, like a chameleon.

I didn't always have a hate for her. I loved her dearly. I suppose I don't hate her; I don't understand how people can lie. I also do not understand the lack of protection for your children. But she was still my mom. It is interesting how kids who are abused still love their parents. We still long for their approval, for their love. Thinking that if we could be better kids, maybe then they will love us.

I do not have many memories of her from my early childhood. I know I tried to cuddle with her often, and she would brush me off. I do not remember her holding me or holding my brothers. I do not think she had the capability to give physical love. She enjoyed playing frisbee, and I lost several teeth trying to play with her. She enjoyed fishing, and she loved scary movies and Stephen King books. She was always reading. She was an exceptional artist, and I was consumed with trying to be as good as she was. I never achieved it, but my daughter did.

As I grew up, the tension between us grew harsher. We never saw eye to eye. We rarely had time together that was pleasant. We fought all the time, as I saw her as a liar, and she saw me as a problem. This conflict is one reason that I chose not to live with her after I left Albert. This is the reason I couch-hopped from age sixteen to nineteen.

My friends loved her. They saw her as a cool mom. She would let us go out all night. We would come home from cruising Main Street in Purcell at midnight, as my friends all had curfews, she would call their moms to say we were home. Then she hung up the phone after talking to their moms and would tell us to go and have fun.

It hurt, standing there, looking at her. I was jealous that my friends had moms who cared where they were. My mom never seemed to care, or at least it felt like she didn't. Maybe to others, she was the cool mom. To me, it felt like she wanted me to fail. She wanted me to do something wrong. She expected me to do something wrong. I desperately wanted my mom to care about me.

Graduation fast approaching, I was one and a half credits short of graduating. Having everything except electives, they allowed me to walk in graduation. Scared but excited, I walked across the stage a year later than my peers my age. I eagerly waited at the end of the stage for photographs, except no one was there to take my picture. The girl at the bottom of the stairs asked me to move so she could get a photo of her little brother, who was behind me. Embarrassed, I moved. After it was over, my mother found me in the crowd. I questioned her presence and why she didn't take a picture. She just said, "It's not like you were really graduating." Defeated, I felt another piece of me die, as did more of my respect for her.

I remember being younger, and she would tell me stories of her childhood, and I would sit and listen as though they were the only history that mattered. She grew up poor. They lived on land and often played outside. She was kicked by a horse, and it took the skin off her elbows. She claimed she had appendicitis as a kid. She said that she and her sisters were caught shaving their faces, and their mom told them that they would grow a full beard from doing so. She then said her dad stepped in and told them not to worry that he'd pluck all the hairs out for them.

She described getting new clothes from Goodwill one year, and she was happy to have gained a new skirt that had comics on it. She proudly wore it to school the next day, and one of the other girls came up to her and made fun of her because she had donated that skirt to Goodwill the day before. I remember being angry and wishing I could punch the girl who hurt her. Sadly, I will never know if her stories were real.

Her mom was an alcoholic. My Aunt Lois told me that their mom had tried to leave their dad before their brothers were born. Maybe she knew something was wrong with that man. My aunt remembered being on a bus with their clothes packed in brown paper bags. One of the bags fell over, and a bottle of liquor rolled out of it. Their time away from their dad was short-lived as they ended up back at his house. I cannot imagine how any woman could take care of three small girls by herself in the 1950s.

Her mom died in 1969. She was forty-three years old. She died of alcoholism. My mom would claim this is why she did not like drinking alcohol. I understood it. I believe she was telling me the truth. I wonder what horrors her mom had endured to give up on life and drink herself to death so young.

I wanted my mom to love me. I tried to be a good kid. Once I came back from Albert, it seemed nothing I did was ever good enough. Maybe it was like that before Albert, and I didn't see it. I was called a selfish bitch a lot. I never understood how a parent could dislike one of their kids.

Maybe this was normal when she was growing up. She would tell me that she and her sister, Lois, would make fun of their other sister, Linda, and say she was the trash man's kid. Maybe having competition with other women was normal. I still do not understand that aspect of life.

I saw her approval on her deathbed. I am a lucky one. I was given a glimpse of love and approval, and thus I was given closure. I pray that others have this opportunity. It is what I try to coach the loved one whose family members have been given a grave prognosis.

Find that common ground to get closure. It does not have to be in a brutal or ugly way. Sometimes, the hurt does come out as yelling. Sometimes, we grieve so deeply for the life we feel we lost and are losing that anger takes over. As they slip from this life into their eternal depth, we feel like we are once again being deprived of something we longed for.

She was frail. Her hair, gone. She weighed a mere eighty-five pounds when she passed. I sat next to her bed before she died, watching her, studying her. I rubbed my hands on her legs to remember how her skin felt; it had stubble. I held her hand and studied her fingers, tenting from dehydration. I rubbed my hand over her head to remember how soft her hair was. I kissed her forehead often so she would know she was loved in her last moments. I moistened her lips and encouraged her to drink. All the evilness, the darkness, and the hurt were gone. She was my mom. My heart anguished within me as the hope I had faded, and I started praying for mercy for her. She suffered for so long. I wanted it to end. I wanted her to hurt no longer, and I wanted to hurt no longer.

She had taken her last breath, her neck now relaxed. I bent over to kiss her forehead one last time after I came back in from the backyard. She was cold; I jerked away. How could she be so cold in such a short period of time? We called the hospice nurse and waited for what felt like eternity drifting by. I waited in my desert: alone in my head, alone in my life. The coping mechanism of shutting out everyone had started. I no longer desired people. I wanted solace.

In her best effort to get the last practical joke in, Larry was standing in the doorway of her room, gazing upon the body of his best friend, whom he had just washed, fed, and taken care of for three weeks; her body sat straight up. He jumped higher than a cat, and I laughed. She had achieved the best and last joke on him.

My father came from Arkansas, and her brothers and sisters gathered to say goodbye. We planned a funeral and buried her in the ground. She was buried in Lexington, a place I can visit her and Trulie's grave, as they are not too far apart, which is quite ironic, as I had lived with Trulie as I learned how to live again after my mom had passed.

So many hours spent at my mom's grave, talking to her grave with just a body. Her soul departed months ago. I cried out to God to take away the pain, to take away the anger. I was so angry. Why? Why did I have to go through more pain in my life? Why must life always be hard? Why did I have to live a life without a mother? I had already lived most of my childhood without a mother.

After months, the visits to her grave became less and less. The pain was still present like a stinging mosquito bite that was scratched too long and too hard. The numbness began to fade, and life started to flourish in its place. When we experience grief, whether expected or not, sometimes we need rest. This gives our body and our minds time to sort out what is necessary.

A month after my mom had passed, I had a friend in Arkansas whose mom had passed suddenly. At that time, I lived in Texas with my second husband, Marty. We were struggling with our marriage because, let's face it, I was already broken, and now I was shattered. I drove the ten-hour drive to Arkansas to be with her during her time of grieving. That is important, as my friends were lifesavers for me during my time of grieving.

I was lying in the spare bedroom of my dad's smoke-filled house, trying to sleep, trying to feel. I finally fell asleep and felt a hand on my shoulder. Angry, I thought that it was my husband, Marty, trying to wake me up for what he thought was "fun" time. I shrugged off the hand. It came again; this time, I rolled over to tell him to leave me alone. As I rolled to my left and onto my back, this was when I remembered—I was in Arkansas, and he was in Texas.

Behind her was a bright light. Peace. A peace that cannot be explained with words enveloped me. Two people stood behind her. They had long hair and had blue sashes on their robes. Their faces were cast down, but she was beautiful.

Before me was my mom. She had a head full of hair. She was strong, and a smile was on her face. She grabbed my upper body in her arms and said, "It's going to be OK." I believed her. How could I not, with this peace that surpassed all understanding, clinging to every fiber of my being? She was whole, and I was able to see how whole she was.

This was not my first encounter with the spiritual realm. When I was married to the sociopath, Albert, I laid out in the sun for several hours. At fifteen, I was quite immature and did not fully understand the consequences of my actions. I proceeded to go inside the house to cool off; I was as red as a lobster.

Our bathroom had a wasp problem, and there were dead wasps on the ground. I sat on the toilet and put my head in my hands. I was so hot. I looked at the bathtub. It was an old metal one and I knew it would be cool if I laid on that metal. It was the last thing I remembered until I saw my body on the ground. It lay around the bottom of the toilet, encircling the toilet, between the bathtub and the toilet. I hovered above it thinking, "Why was I lying there? There were wasps there." I thought that I wouldn't like that. In an instance, I was back in my body, lying exactly as I saw myself when hovering above. I was certain that I had just had a brief near-death experience, and I became afraid.

I clumsily dragged myself to the kitchen and began drinking water. I knew a doctor was not in question, so I waited patiently for Albert to come home from work. My body was aching from dry, stretched skin caused by a severe sunburn. I kept my experience to myself, afraid that others would think I was crazy.

It was not until I became a full-fledged Christian that I spoke of either of these events. I know some people would say that I am making it up. It's not unusual for others to say that I am seeking attention. I am now telling my story for others. If you have experienced something similar, it's ok. People do not need to believe you. God gave you a gift to see something others only dream of seeing. Harbor that experience if it was a good one. If you feel it was a bad one, I encourage you to look deep. Do you have a relationship with Jesus? Are you certain where you would go if you died?

God is Good

God always has a way of showing up when you need Him. Three weeks before my mom passed away, she was inpatient in the hospital. A social worker had called to ask me if we could take her in for hospice. I was working full-time, and my second husband, Marty, was working full-time. She needed twenty-four-hour care and, if we took her in, one of us would have to quit our jobs, and we would not be able to pay our bills.

Frustrated and upset, I hung up the phone and cried. The phone immediately rang, and it was one of my mom's coworkers, Larry. He said the Lord just told him that I needed him. I explained my dilemma, and without hesitation, he said he would take her in. He rented a house from his parents and moved her in within twenty-four hours. He took care of her every night after work, and his mom took care of her during the day. I went over after work several times a week to provide relief.

One day, Larry said he was standing at the kitchen sink when a cold wind swept past him. He ran to my mom's room, as he thought she had passed away. He said that she looked over at him and said, "My demons have left me." This was about four days before she passed away.

When my mom was taking her last breath, I got up from her bedside and ran out of the room. I wanted to be there for her, but at the same time, everything in me was telling me to run away. Marty and Larry sat with her and held her hand as she died.

Once I had left that room, I went out back to where my stepdad, Charlie, was sitting out by the fence. He was sitting under the most beautiful wisteria. I curled up beside him and lay my head on his shoulder. Without saying a word, he knew and burst into tears. He got up and made his way inside. I still sat there trying to feel... something.

I remained numb for five months. I do not recall many memories in those five months, except the horrible, intense urge to pick up the phone and call my mom. Those awful, dreadful flashbacks would arrive completely out of the blue and smack me in the face—of her writhing in pain, screaming out, gasping for air. She died like a fish out of water. To this day, I hate the sound of an oxygen home actuator. It reminds me of her death.

At the end of those five months, after my mom passed away, I traveled back to Oklahoma to see my friend Trulie. I was living in Texas at the time. This is when I left Marty. After the visit with Trulie, I decided to move back to Oklahoma and be a nanny for the Chronister girls. Another memory during those five months was the letters that the Chronister girls' dad allowed them to send me. I loved them dearly. These three precious girls entered my life while I was a two-year-old teacher at a daycare. I watched them often for their dad. I loved them and they loved me. Once I was back in their lives, and they in mine, I had purpose.

Two years later, my dad left his life in Arkansas to be closer to Philip and me. It was at that time that Philip and I started college to prepare for nursing school. We lived with our dad during this time. We were accepted and graduated together. We had been inspired by the many great nurses who took exceptional care of our mother. Also, I, this barren woman, bore my first child, Max. He is my first precious gift from God.

I do not know if Philip and James knew the extent of my trauma, but I suspect that they have their own story. My dad was told of what happened to me, and he apologized for not protecting me.

My Dad

When I was around four, my dad picked us up from Aunt Linda's. We moved to the country with our new stepmom, Piggy, and my stepsister. We had a garden, and it was the first time I ate fried squash. I still do not like fried squash.

We had ducks, chickens, and dogs. We played outside as kids all the time. We would play Cowboys and Indians or The Dukes of Hazzard. I always wanted to be Daisy Duke, but I always ended up being Boss Hogg's wife, which is quite funny now.

My dad was a mechanic and had his shop on the land. I spent a lot of time in his shop with him, as I did throughout my life. I know a lot about cars and how to fix them. I was always Daddy's little girl. My nickname was "Sissy" until my little sister came along. I gladly passed it down to her, and then my oldest niece received that nickname. She still has it to this day, and she's forty.

My favorite thing to do was ride with my daddy in his truck, right next to him with my little hand holding his arm. I always felt safe when he was around. Then one day, he took a job as a long-distance truck driver. My time to see him grew more and more apart. I would cry at night if I heard his truck leave and if I didn't get to see him.

Finally, when I was in kindergarten, my mom showed up with yet another stepdad and took us away. We did not go to live with her—instead, she dropped us off at Wanda and Tommy's, but eventually she came back to take us home with her.

This stepdad was kind. He was the one invested in us. My dad's visits grew further and further apart. When it was time for him to come and get us, we would sit on the front porch. Hours would creep by until the darkness would succumb upon us, and the stars would shine bright. I remember seeing the Milky Way in the Oklahoma night sky. My dad never showed up.

With the negative comments piling on from our mother, we all began to hate our dad and began to cling more to the stepdad. He stepped in when our dad stepped out. For a year in school, we took his last name. I can't blame that man for running. He was thrust into a lot of responsibility, and I'm sure he signed on to have my mom.

Living with my dad was not all roses. This was the first place where I saw real physical abuse. My stepmom beat James, Philip, and her daughter with whatever she could grab. If there were nothing handy, she would use her fists. I never remember her beating me. I remember being spanked with a belt for crying for my daddy once but never being beaten. Maybe it happened, and it's somewhere in the depths of my mind, afraid to emerge. I doubt that, though. For some reason, she seemed to like me.

I also had a strange food aversion as a child. I gagged at different textures easily, and if forced to continue to eat whatever it was, I vomited. That brought a lot of spankings my way whenever I was not with my dad. My stepmom never spanked me for it. I just had to go to bed hungry. I went to bed hungry a lot, with my little tummy hurting from hunger pains.

One night, it was spaghetti night. I loved spaghetti. I was the last one at the table: only kids sat at the table. My stepsister told me not to eat my spaghetti because James had put a booger in it. I cried. My dad was mad. I'm sure that they were tired of me not eating. My dad got up from his chair, grabbed my plate of spaghetti, and started eating it, cussing between bites.

My brothers and sister fell silent. I could tell by the looks on their faces that something was up. James had a look of shock on his face, and slowly nodding his head yes, said, "I really did put a booger in your spaghetti." I used that story twenty years later for a college English paper and made a crisp 100% on it. Reading it to my dad, I realized that it was the first time he had heard that he did, in fact, eat James' booger. He started cussing, and I laughed the biggest belly laugh my tiny adult self could laugh. Oh, good times.

He was not the best dad in the world, but he was my dad. This little girl loved her dad immensely. He did things for me as a child, such as letting me eat the crispy part off the fried chicken because I didn't like the texture of the chicken, just the crunchy outside. He would then take the chicken I had left, mangled, and eat the meat inside. He never complained about it. He cussed! Oh, did he cuss.

When my little sister Jill was three years old, she was standing in the middle seat of the Suburban—because that was what you needed when you had a ton of kids in the 1980s—and she started cussing like a sailor. My dad, angry as a beaver, started cussing himself. And somewhere in all that cussing was a, "Who taught her that?" We giggled in the back seat, knowing it was him and thinking it was funny that he could not see his error.

I love my little sister. She came into my life when I was five years old. After not being able to see my little brother Bobby very much, I longed for another baby to be nearby. Piggy brought her home, and I was in love. They placed her in what appeared to be a Mama Roo nowadays. This crazy contraption had to be adjusted by pushing the top part forward and moving a metal bar in the back to adjust the height. I had seen the adults do it, so my determined self thought that I could do it too.

The problem was that Jill was not strapped in. She was sitting on the coffee table in her little yellow seat. I was leaning forward, trying to get right in her face. I was too short. I proceeded to push the top part forward. I moved the bar and happily marched myself to the front of the seat. She wasn't there. She was on the ground, face first, and she was screaming. I quickly picked her up as my stepmom came around the corner. I had dropped my sister on her head. Sorry, Jill, whatever is wrong with you may be my fault. Just kidding, she is a wonderful lady.

My Dad Later in Life

My dad's dad was an alcoholic. He beat my dad and his brothers. My uncle followed suit and started drinking at a young age. My uncle drowned his sorrows until he died in 2019.

My dad drank, but it was not like my uncle. I remember him drinking a beer after work when I was young but not becoming a slobbering drunk like his brother. One amazing thing about both was their ability to work on cars.

My dad was a certified Toyota mechanic, and he could listen to a car over the phone and tell you exactly what was wrong with it. My uncle could do body work that looked as though the car was brand new, even when he was a non-functional alcoholic.

My dad broke the alcoholic generational curse for his kids but passed along the broken family curse. He never got to see his kids grow and leave home for a marriage. He also moved from woman to woman, having more kids. We tried to visit him throughout the years, as he moved from state to state, but a woman always warranted his time away from us.

He had his favorite children, and we all knew it. I was an exceptionally troubled teenager after I escaped the Sociopath. I was hell bent on self-destruction. One summer, I visited my dad. That summer was full of irresponsible fun and lessons learned.

I learned how to drink, steal, and smoke pot. I was sixteen and a half years old. I learned to grab the chair in front of the box fan in the window at night to sleep. No air conditioning? A box fan in a window on a summer night in the Arkansas mountains made everything better.

I learned how to siphon gas, steal lunchmeat from the grocery store, and bathe while boiling water on the wood stove. I also learned that this lifestyle was dangerous. I bounced between Arkansas and Oklahoma, couch surfing for over two years. Then I finally decided I needed to try to finish high school.

Although my dad allowed Philip, my older brother, to live with him while he finished high school, I was too much trouble. I wasn't allowed to stay with him, partly because of his girlfriend, who did not like me, and she was dead set on me not staying with them; the other part was that I was a troubled teenager. I ended up at my best friend's house in Lexington. I am so thankful for her mom, from whom I mimic a lot of my own mom skills. Norma Beason, you raised a good woman in me, thank you.

When my dad became older, his frailty was rigid. Living with Chronic Obstructive Pulmonary Disease, or COPD, from exposure to ammonia in the Vietnam War, he could barely walk without being out of breath. When he was around the age of seventy-five, he became sick and contracted Clostridium difficile infection, or C-diff. He was discharged from the hospital but never regained any strength.

Since he needed care around the clock, and I could only see him twice a week because I was working two full-time jobs, he placed himself in a nursing home. He chose one in Lexington. When I say he chose the poorest nursing home to live in, I say it with full truth. I rarely saw the floors clean. But he was happy there.

He stayed in that facility for over a year before he decided to move to the VA center in Norman, Oklahoma. It was clean, and the food was good. I would visit and take him the things he would ask for, like Dr Pepper or snacks. Sometimes I would help him in the wheelchair, take him to the cafeteria, and we would eat dinner together.

Did I mention that my dad was a grumpy old man? Ah, yes, the grumpy old man syndrome. He complained every second I was with him. One of the most negative people I have ever met in my life. I would sigh and listen to story after story of those who did him wrong in his life, again and again. I loved him still.

When his seventy-eighth birthday rolled around, I knew it would be his last. I gathered six of the nine children who bore his last name. These six kids were, in fact, his biological kids. We threw him a surprise party.

We gathered in the sitting area right outside his room. I went in, helped him into his wheelchair, and told him he needed to come out to the sitting area. As I wheeled him out of his room, there were all six of his kids, and most of his grandkids, waiting to wish him a happy birthday. In front of all of us, my dad placed his face in his hands and wept.

Picture this: six kids, all with the same introverted trait. Sitting with their children, all with the same introverted trait. It was the quietest party I have ever been to. I have pictures, I have memories, and I know I did everything I could for that grumpy old man while he was alive. That was in the year 2020. His birthday was in January. On March 14th, 2020, the nursing center closed its doors to keep its residents safe. I kissed his forehead and thought I would see him again in two weeks.

I dropped off his snacks and Dr Pepper, as he demanded. I talked on the phone as much as he wanted. Then one day, I got a call from the head nurse that my dad was lethargic. He was a DNR (do not resuscitate), and I respected his wishes, but I also knew that if it was just pneumonia, he could be treated.

I sent him to the ER. My dad weighed 121 pounds when I last saw him in March, and by early May, when he was in the ER, he had dropped to 104 pounds. Philip and I were unsure if it was sarcopenia or possibly just an illness. One thing is for sure, while he was in the hospital for a week, he had gained weight and gone back up to 114 pounds.

Concerned that the facility was not feeding him correctly, since I could not visit and ensure everything was in order, I called and spoke with the dietitian. She stated that she could do nothing and that it was up to the nurses to ensure that he was eating. My hands were tied.

My dad went back to the nursing home. He called me on May 28th to say his phone would not stay charged and he needed a new phone charger. I was working a twelve-hour shift and would not be off until 7:00 p.m.

After leaving work in Bethany, Oklahoma, I drove home, picked up an extra charger, and drove to the east side of Norman to drop it off for my dad. I called him on his phone and told him that I had dropped it off and that I loved him.

The next day, on May 29th, my little sister Jill called me around 4:00 p.m. to say that Dad would not answer his phone. Thinking that the charger I dropped off must not have worked, I called the nurse supervisor and asked her to take her phone to my dad so that I could talk to him. She was too busy but said she would later.

I got off work at 7:00 p.m. and called again. I had a male nurse this time, who insisted that they would have him call. I called again an hour later, still no luck. At 9:00 p.m., I received a call from the Veterans Center. It was the male nurse from earlier, asking if my dad had called. I said, "No, I haven't heard from him." He plainly said, "Well, he's dead." Thinking that they must have the wrong patient, I double checked the names. It was, in fact, my dad. I broke. I cried out in pain. Everything in my being thought that I was supposed to be with him when he passed, like I did for my mom, but I let him die alone. I felt like I had failed him.

I called all my siblings to tell them, but I could only reach Philip. He and his son Tim went to the Center to say goodbye; Philip called me to say that he looked peaceful. Dad had died peacefully in his sleep. We were unsure if he died the night before or that day. His phone was dead, so I suspected that it was the night before.

We had a small funeral in June 2020, and I officiated. It was just how that grumpy old man would have wanted it. He had one friend show up. We gathered as siblings and laughed about the fact that all he ever fed us was bologna sandwiches, fried chicken, or pizza. We laughed about how much he cussed. We laughed about the fact that we were all so much like him, with his intelligence and stubbornness.

Bobby

Bobby was young when he quit coming to Dad's on the weekends. He had a little brother named Charlie who had been coming with him. For the longest time, I didn't know why he stopped coming to see Dad. I thought about him often while I was growing up.

One day, I found out that my sister, Gena, knew where his mom was living. I asked her to ask if I could come and see Bobby. At this time, I was sixteen and he was fourteen. I was permitted with the stipulation that I was not to tell my dad where they lived. I agreed.

Ecstatic, I picked up Jill and we went to see our long-lost brother. It had been over ten years since I had seen him. Charlie sat on the couch; he seemed full of life and happy to see us. Bobby sat on a chair in the kitchen. His expression was not inviting. He would not speak. He only glared from his seat.

Although I tried to give Charlie attention, I kept looking back at Bobby. Drawn to this young man, like our souls were always intertwined since the day he was brought home from the hospital. Deep down, I knew Charlie was not my brother, although his mom had claimed he was. There is a deep-rooted connection between my dad's biological kids—poor Charlie did not possess it.

Bobby never reciprocated the attention afforded to him. It would be years before we saw him again. This time, he would be around twenty-two years old. My dad lived in Purcell at the time, and I had reconnected with Bobby, convincing him to come and have dinner with us. He did, but my dad had a new woman in his life, and his attention was on her. We were upset with him for having his priorities mixed up. We lost touch again for several years.

One day, Bobby reached out and expressed interest in forming a relationship. It was hit or miss for several years. We eventually lost touch again until around 2012. We have remained close. I love him dearly. I love his wife and their boys.

He was able to have a relationship with our dad as well before our dad passed. I remember when Bobby traveled to see Dad in his nursing home in Lexington. I think having that relationship with him gave our dad the spirit needed to continue living. He made it for two more years before he passed away peacefully in his sleep.

CHAPTER SIX

Like a Diamond Being Rescued from the Coal

Proud

No one tells you that they're proud of you, coming from a traumatic childhood; you crave the words that were never afforded to you as a child. Every child wants their parents to see them. That's why they are continually in front of their parent saying, "Look at me!" or "Watch this!" When I was in my early twenties after my mom passed away, I lived with my childhood best friend. Trulie was three kids deep, and I was barren at the time. Being with her and getting to help raise her kids was what my broken heart needed.

Her two oldest children were somewhat unruly. I tried the reverse psychology method with her oldest son, telling him how proud I was of him after he had done something good, rather than constantly reprimanding him for doing something wrong.

Slowly, it started to work, and his behavior began changing, until the day he turned to his mom after I had told him I was proud of him. With his sweet little voice, he looked her in the face and said, "Are you proud of me, Mama?" My heart broke. It does help when others say it, but what we really desire is to hear it from our mother. Instead of getting the reaction he desired, she became mad at me for starting the whole "I am proud of you" movement.

Into my adulthood and middle age, I craved the words, "I'm so proud of you." From every parent figure, every so-called friend, every in-law. The problem is that I realized words and actions never aligned. The more I strived to be successful, the more the ones who should have loved me pulled away, and other people drew closer.

When my daughter was sixteen, she wanted to join me at Royal Family Kids Camp. I was ecstatic. I wanted to share my passion with my only daughter. It was her interview for the camp that opened my eyes to my subconscious desire for someone to be proud of me.

During the interview, she was asked to name her hero. Without hesitation, she said her mom, "Because she has achieved everything she has set out to do; nothing stops her." In an instant, it gave me an "aha" moment for the years of lack of love. My greatest cheerleaders are my kids. I was a mother whom they were proud of.

Liars

When we were growing up, Trulie would say to her little brother, "You lie, you fry." Her mom would get so upset. She was right, though. As stated in the Holy Bible, Revelation 21:8, "But cowards, unbelievers, the corrupt, murderers, the immoral, those who practice witchcraft, idol worshippers, and all liars—their fate is in the fiery lake of burning sulfur. This is the second death."

As a child, I was a little liar. I lied for no reason at all. Then one day, James broke his school ruler. He blamed it on me. I didn't break it, but no one believed me. It felt horrible not to be believed. I strived not to lie after that; it took a long time to break that generational curse, and now I am the worst liar.

My mother, on the other hand, pulled the wool over so many people's eyes. The family would call and invite us to family gatherings, and she would tell them we would be there and hang up. I would get so excited, thinking I was going to see my cousins, just to have her say that she only said that so that they would shut up and leave her alone. This is probably why I hate getting my hopes up, because getting them let down sucks.

When my mom's hair fell off when I was a little girl, my family told me that she had a brain tumor and that she lost her hair while undergoing chemo. This was when getting rid of us was the most important task. I asked my mom about that brain tumor when she was sick with lung cancer. She laughed and said she never had a brain tumor. She had dyed her hair too much, and her hair fell out.

You see, it's hard to remember lies. People lie to get what they want. Selfish individuals will go to great lengths to achieve their goals. My aunt told me that my mom was treated for cancer for over a year. My aunt had suspicions that my mom was lying at the time, but did not want to accuse her of lying if it was, in fact, cancer.

My mom had people take her to appointments, but would not let them go in. She received money from all her friends and relatives using the excuse of "cancer" to fuel sympathy. Now, here we are, twenty years later, and it was all a lie.

Recently, I had a conversation with Philip about this. He did not know it was a lie. I think he was in disbelief and thought I was wrong about it all. If I had not been the one to have the conversation with my mom, I would probably be in disbelief as well.

After Mom passed, my stepdad found out that my mom was trying to get a loan on their land that they both owned, in her name alone. He also thought that he was her second husband and had no idea about the other five or so. Lying is such a bad trait, and not one that belongs in a life that desires peace. The devil shows up in lies voiced by others.

Psychology

At the age of twenty-one, I started college. It was interesting to walk into a college, even if it was a community college. I had obtained my GED and was excited to experience what college would hold.

The counselor suggested a slew of classes that I felt were not relevant to the medical field. One was a class to learn how to speak properly. I guess the country Okie slang was not appropriate for the normal city person. I politely declined the extra courses and focused on what was required and what I considered necessary.

One of the requirements for nursing school was a course in psychology. The professor asked how many hours of sleep people in class got every night. He said, "Raise your hand if you get less than six hours a night." This was a sign of anxiety.

Then, he asked about seven to eight hours of sleep, which was a normal sleeping pattern. Then, he moved on to nine hours, and at last, ten hours or more. I was the only one who raised their hand at ten hours or more. Slightly embarrassed, I slowly lowered my hand. I could tell by the look on his face—the look I seriously dreaded from everyone. It was as if he had read my past like a book. I stayed in the back of the class from that point on. I was afraid of him asking more questions or bringing out more of my secrets.

He was a good professor, or perhaps I was so ignorant of real life that I absorbed all the knowledge that spewed from his mouth, taking it in and being healed by it. He explained that ninety-three percent of people are not thinking about others. Let me explain. If you walk into a room and you are immediately worried about what others are thinking, know that ninety-three percent of those people are only thinking about themselves. They are afraid of being judged. They are wondering about their lives. They are wondering if they fit in, if others like them.

Only a small percentage think about other people. This does not necessarily mean that what they are thinking is negative. A rare few are givers; people who continually think about other people. They are complimenting you in their heads. They are reading your pain and silently praying for you. There are good people in the world.

The downfall is that these people who are givers, if they have not healed the broken parts of themselves, they can be sucked dry by the other ninety-three percent. They try to heal everyone around them. They can be broken by giving too much of themselves until they are empty shells. This is why psychology is not a good career choice for givers. They will take on the pain of others and take it home, causing trouble in their personal lives.

Therapy

Therapy is a crazy thing. Stepping into a room with a total stranger and releasing the skeletons from your closet; it was such an odd yet needed task, at least it was for me. My therapy adventure was quite interesting. If you knew me back then as a young adult, you wouldn't recognize me now.

Picture a shy girl whose face turns bright red with embarrassment when her name is called out. Now throw in the shame of sexual abuse, and you have one withdrawn young lady.

I ended up in therapy because I had gotten married, and I was twenty-one years old. It was my second marriage. I genuinely enjoyed his company, but when the wedding day came, I wanted to run away. It was not cold feet; it was fear that he would see my shame, think I was disgusting, or worse, think I was trash.

On my wedding day, I told my mom that I wanted to back out. Her words still ring in my head, "He's the best you'll ever get." Due to a combination of looking at my frail mom who was wasting away from the cancerous tumors spreading throughout her body, wanting to please her, wanting her to see me get married before she died, and going between the fact that she may be right, I married him.

Who would want me? The broken, weird, shy girl? I always thought that I was ugly; therefore, she must have been right. We married, and during the honeymoon, I could not shake the thought that I had made a terrible mistake.

Thus, comes therapy. He suggested therapy, I suggested divorce. I did not win. I began calling counselors, and in 1995, the cost was over $100 per visit. Quite crazy considering we made $20,000 a year together. Neither one of our jobs offered insurance, so we needed a different solution.

Somehow, I ended up calling the University of Oklahoma's (OU) counseling center. Students staffed it, and the counselors were third- and fourth-year students. The sessions were only $5.

My interview was lengthy, around two hours long. They only had a few spots open, and they needed subjects that the students could use as teaching models. I sat in a sterile room with only two chairs and a two-way mirror. I was informed that I was being recorded, and although I prayed in my head that no one who knew me would ever see those videos, I consented.

It was a different experience. Have you ever heard about someone feeling like they were in a tunnel? I experienced this. Staring at the person doing my intake, sharing my deep, dark secrets. It felt like someone else was talking, as though I was not there.

I must have made an impact, as I qualified for one of the openings, and they wanted me back the following week. They had a student who wanted to take on my case. I saw her two times a week for ten months. I do not remember her giving me much advice; she mainly listened. Maybe that was what I needed, or maybe I needed someone to listen, who didn't call me a liar or didn't look at me like I was broken.

This was not the first time I had opened up about my past sexual abuse. The first time was with my best friend, Trulie, when I was eleven. I felt heard and not judged. At the age of seventeen, I confided in another best friend. She immediately ran to my mom and told her. I had never told my mom before that day. My mom told my friend that I was a liar, just looking for attention. I didn't tell anyone again until my second husband, and he could barely get any information out of me.

Trust was hard for me, still is. Maybe that's why I clung to that early childhood best friend. I never felt judged by her; she was always loving, open, and caring. I felt accepted.

This eager soul who agreed to take on my case, in counseling, lived on a roller coaster with me. I've always had very vivid dreams. To this day, I still have prophetic dreams. The dreams that followed my therapy were disturbing. Throughout my healing journey, every dream was centered around that house, Grandpa's house. The broken-down white house on the Southside of Oklahoma City. Sexual abuse happened in every room, so I knew that house inside and out.

The smells, colors, and everything that should already be forgotten linger in my mind with each traumatic event, like rotting wood. The bedroom with the frilly comforter and Avon bottles stacked on the dresser. The second bedroom had a señorita doll sitting on the bed, which I was not allowed to play with. The back closet was lined with old clothes—a great place to take an innocent child to violate without anyone seeing. His chair in the living room sat facing the window to the driveway. It was the perfect place to make a child fondle you while you watched for anyone to return, so you would not be caught. The couch behind his recliner was where I slept when I was tired. The weird plastic grapes on the coffee table I used to like to squish flat, but I always got into trouble for touching them. And that nasty, dark kitchen, where the roaches resided and fled when the lights came on.

People may ask, "Why didn't you tell someone? Why did you keep going around him?" Very good questions. I didn't tell anyone because I loved him, and I truly believed that he loved me. I was his "favorite," and I had never felt like anyone's favorite before.

I felt like no one wanted me around except my brothers. None of the other family members acted like they liked me either. I remember being at Grandpa's house, and one of our uncles came over. He immediately started wrestling with my brothers, but he pushed me away. A hard push. A not-so-loving push, and I didn't know why. As I got older, those memories made me feel more broken. The child molester was the only one who loved me.

I kept going because my mom kept taking me. Around the age of eight, I started saying I didn't want to go. I had come to the enlightenment that what he did to me was wrong. I didn't want to be around him any longer, so I avoided him.

Sometimes, I still had to go. He was weak, his body ravaged by cancer, the only saving grace for my younger cousins. I would cringe when he held them in his lap. I would pray that he couldn't hurt them, wondering if anyone knew the bad things he had done to me and, if they did, how they could place their baby girls in his lap.

He was always sitting in the recliner. He had lost his voice box to cancer, and they had removed one of his lungs, so that side of his chest was sunken in. He looked like walking death long before he died. Using a machine to talk to everyone that sounded like a robot, and everyone would laugh and talk about his new voice.

In my dreams, I was a little girl again, and grandpa was an adult. Sometimes in my dreams, I wanted his approval, so I allowed sexual abuse to happen, enjoying watching him being happy, just as it had been in real life.

I was just a small, little girl who wanted to make her grandpa happy, not knowing right from wrong, and not knowing the extensive psychological effects it would have on me later in life. Then, as therapy advanced, I became a grown woman in my dreams. He was frail before me, and I found a voice. I told him, "No," in my dreams. I told him he had no power over me and took back a part of me I had left in that house when I was little.

That house burned to the ground not long after he died. I think it was justice. It held such an evil history for me. The flashback would have been too much, too tormenting if I had to go back to that house many times after he died.

The young student counselor asked me one day, "What will you do as a parent to ensure your children will not go through what you went through?" It was simple, I knew exactly what I would do. Something no one did for me. "I would make sure they had a voice." If my children always felt heard and worthy, they would never feel ashamed to talk to their mom.

I still wonder if those videos of me from counseling are used to this day. I'm unique in the sense that I should not have made it. My story is compelling; it probably follows the plot of many others out there.

Maybe I was lucky and had a great student. She asked me to do something outside of therapy during one session and report back how it went. It was something that looked simple, but to me, it was not.

My student counselor asked me to tell my aunt and uncles about my abuse. Wow! Seems simple enough, right? Go to the living children of the man who sexually abused me and tell them that their dad was a monster.

When my grandpa died, I stayed with one of my uncles and his family. I walked by his room and saw him sitting on his bed, holding a picture of his dad, and sobbing uncontrollably. So, to heal, I had to hurt others?

How does one do this? Wouldn't it just be easier to keep the secret and live with it? What if they called me a liar like my mom did? What if they hated me? This was tough because I was someone who just wanted to be loved and accepted. It's like placing stones around you in a circle, then standing there, telling the people you love the truth, closing your eyes, and waiting for them to throw stones at you. But which is worse—their abuse or the abuse that you've been hiding?

I decided to go to the one person I felt would listen to me, my Aunt Lois. I loved her and trusted her, so I made my move and asked her if we could talk. Have you ever been out in the backyard of an old house, and you thought that you had found some hidden treasure barely sticking out of the ground? You start digging and digging, and your excitement grows like embers burning in a raging fire until you reach the bottom of the treasure and find out that you had just dug up a buried thirty-five-year-old hatchet?

Yes, that's what I did. I told my aunt that her dad had violated me sexually, and she hung her head. Not the reaction I had expected.

She said that she was sorry and then proceeded to tell me HER story. Perhaps her story ultimately contributed to my overall healing process. I looked back and realized that my story was not as bad as hers. She was ten years old when she was plucked out of bed. Fourteen years old when she left home. She was not sure how old she was when he first had intercourse with her, but she said it happened. She also knew that it had happened to her sisters, even though they never talked about it.

She expressed her anger at her sisters for leaving her, as they left as young teens to escape the hell they were living. She was the youngest and the last girl to leave home. And I finally had my answer as to why my mom dropped out of eighth grade.

There I sat, in a booth, across from my aunt in her restaurant. I had to do something with this heavy information I now possessed. I have to say that during my time in therapy, my mom started to decline faster. It wasn't unusual for her to spend weeks in the hospital from extreme weakness. Not only was I healing from my past, but I was also trying to live in an extremely grotesque present. So, how do you confront your weak, fragile mother with this information?

Being the quiet, nonconfrontational twenty-one-year-old that I was, I did what every immature girl would do—I wrote my mom a letter. I let her know everything that man did to me, from simple molestation to trying to have intercourse with a five-year-old child. I let her know that I knew her secret that she and her sisters had hidden. I told her that her sister had told me everything. I ended with how horrible she was to place me in that situation, knowing that he would hurt me.

How could any mother place her child in harm's way? I walked that folded letter into that hospital, up to her room, placed it on her bedside table, and walked away. I could not even speak. I was sick from anger, frustration, and hurt. She called me multiple times a day for three days.

I would not accept her phone call. Frankly, I was shut down emotionally. How do you respond to the one who helped ruin your life? So, I did what I thought was best for me, and I forgave her.

I went to see her around the fourth day after I gave her the letter. She sat in her hospital bed, frail, with hardly any hair. She was solemn and sad. She said that she was sorry; she thought that he had changed. She didn't throw faults or make me feel as though I should have spoken up. She accepted her fate and took the trophy for the world's worst mother.

I'm sure that my face was not inviting, but I did love her. It was at that moment that I saw my options—I could choose closure, or I could choose to live in this pain and bitterness for the rest of my life. I chose closure.

She talked about what she went through; I was able to sympathize. She gave me genuine apologies several times and I consumed them. It was as though I met my mom for the first time.

This brings me back to my counselor: a smart, young lady who already knew the answer to her question. She knew that he had done terrible things before. She knew that my mom hid a secret. What floored her was my forgiveness.

What a great experience. This young lady helped me find my voice. She also helped me listen to that small voice. You know, the one that speaks up to keep you out of trouble? Yes, that one. The same one I heard on the day I married my second husband. He did not deserve the jacked-up version of me that he received. He was kind to me and sat with my mom while she took her last breath.

The student counselor also helped me determine that Marty, my second husband, was not right for me. She had me take a test, and then Marty took a test. I am not sure what the name of that test was, as it was so long ago. The results: we were incompatible. Not just a little bit, but a lot. She did not encourage me to divorce, but said if it did happen, she would not be shocked.

Ultimately, we were not meant to be. We divorced; it was the right thing to do. I needed to heal myself from the past and the present. My mom died a horrible death. Like a fish out of water, she suffocated, gasping for air. More than twenty-four hours of her writhing in bed, screaming out in pain. Her neck was bent to the right, as she had a tumor in her throat that made it hard for her to breathe or swallow. She was a skeleton with pale skin attached to it; she only weighed eighty-five pounds when she passed.

She lost the ability to move her legs two weeks before she died, and they stayed bent, near her chest. I was spent; emotionally, physically, and spiritually. I stood in the doorway, gazing upon my mom, her body contracted with pain. She looked over at me and said these four things:

1. Don't smoke
2. Go to church
3. Get right with God
4. Don't forget me

Imagine being afraid of being forgotten. Maybe it was because her mom died at the age of forty-three, and now my mom was dying at the age of forty-eight. Perhaps she felt like she had forgotten her mom and was afraid that I would forget her, too.

I can still see that memory as clear as day. I took those words to heart. She died that night. We all relaxed. Her pain was over; ours was beginning. We lived the last two years thinking that she would be healed. It was only in the last three weeks of her life that I understood that she was dying. She kept saying that she was going to live. She kept saying that she would be healed. Naive, I believed her.

Perhaps this is why honesty and truthfulness have been my greatest qualities in the healthcare field. When encountering friends or patients' families, I encourage them to spend all the time they can with their family members who have cancer. Do all the things, make the memories, and enjoy them while they are here.

I wish someone had sat me down and explained to me that she would die, I would have tried more. I would have visited her more. I would have answered every phone call. I would have brought her every milkshake she asked for. I learned my lesson well. So, when it came time to be there for my dad, I was fully present.

Expression Of Oneself

On my mom's deathbed, she told me her regrets. One regret was that she wished she had traveled more. She had never left the United States. I think she had many more regrets than this, but this one stuck with me. In 2014, I was offered the opportunity to travel to Swaziland (now known as Eswatini) to assist in building an orphanage. I left my family for ten days and went. I did not and do not want to live with regrets.

After my mom passed away, I was living with Trulie, and I decided that life was way too short for regrets. I also decided that being shy would give me too many regrets. Trulie introduced me to many new people in Purcell in 1996. I knew where a few of them lived. I was bored and she was busy. I decided to drive to one of my new friend's houses and hang out with them.

Scared to death, I knocked on the door. They invited me in. These new friends gave Trulie and me nicknames. We were called Bill and Trustie, and I had no idea why. For about eight months, Bill and Trustie ran the streets of Purcell. People finally knew me. I had an identity of my own; I felt worthy. That little bit of confidence started my journey to becoming who I am.

I could finally talk to strangers without blushing. I made several new friends in college. When I was accepted into nursing school, I had to walk into a stranger's room and engage in conversation. I remembered the movie *Never Been Kissed*, and I related to Josie because she also didn't feel seen. But when she went back to high school, she had an opportunity to "act" like someone else. That is what I did. I chose to act like I wasn't shy that day when I went to my new friend's house back in 1996. Slowly, and through more and more interactions, I could talk to strangers everywhere I went.

This is not how I healed my shame and guilt. Therapy and a kind man helped me heal the trauma of my sexual abuse. This led to my third husband, Chris, being more understanding of boundaries. That is what I needed: to set boundaries to help keep from triggering my PTSD. It's not that I do not get triggered anymore, it's that now, I can talk myself down in my head.

Having someone who respects you when you say, "Do not touch me like that" is more beautiful than the words "I love you." Words are words, and my trust in words is downright next to zero. A big thank you to all the liars for giving me those boundaries. But actions, actions set in motion, are powerful. Someone to sit and listen to when the demons whisper in your ear that you are not good enough. Not to fix you, but to listen. Because when you can talk about it and get it off your chest, it is like the demons lose their power.

I am a highly independent woman and very determined, as well. My determination comes from the fact that I vowed never to depend on a man. Many times, we were hungry or homeless or both because my mom was between men. She had no skills to provide for us. This was why I was determined to finish college and eventually graduate school.

The hard part about being independent is your craving for someone to wrap their arms around you. You desire someone to take care of you, like the child you once were, who needed it so desperately. When someone tries to take care of you, your coping mechanisms kick in, and you get defensive because they think that you cannot do it on your own. Therefore, you try to push them away in an attempt to preserve your independence and strength to sustain yourself. This never-ending fight is continuous. One day, I hope to overcome this darkness within me and truly love and be loved.

Lonely

I was not necessarily a lonely child. I had my brothers; they were there for me. What I craved was adult love and acceptance. Unfortunately, what I was given was an intense feeling of shame and guilt that led me to become a very withdrawn, shy girl. I had no idea how to talk to people. James did most of my talking for me when I was little.

As I got older, I was afraid that if I talked, people would look at me. If they looked at me, maybe they would see it, the shame and guilt. The dirtiness that I carried was like a shroud of dust, similar to the ones seen around Pigpen from the Peanuts comic strip created by Charles M. Schulz. At least, that's what I felt like I looked like.

Always wanting acceptance, I would do stupid stuff like steal or fight if a friend provoked me. Once, my stepsister and her friend were discussing who their favorite person in the family was. We were supposed to be asleep. We were all piled in the living room on pallets. Some on the floor, some on the couch; I had claimed the chair. I do not know if they knew that I was awake at the time—I thought that they thought that I was asleep. As they rated the likability of each person in our family, I was dead last. I was nine or ten years old, and I softly cried myself to sleep. I like to think that they were just being mean girls.

I had friends in high school. Tough friends who protected me. I was able to be myself around them. I was quick-witted and made great comebacks. My friends would come to me to throw shade at other girls' antics. We had fun together, even if I couldn't hang for long. Our best times were spent cruising Main Street in Purcell in Melissa's or April's vehicles. A very tired child, and still am a tired adult, I would curl up in the backseat and sleep while they partied well into the night.

After starting therapy, I had a dream I was at a class reunion. There were life-size cardboard cutouts of each graduate, even though I supposedly graduated a year after all my friends. The objective was to sign each person's cut-out, much like in a yearbook. April's was signed all over, as well as Melissa's and Trulie's. Mine had three signatures: April's, Melissa's, and Trulie's. During the reunion, no one knew my name. They called me Trulie's friend, Melissa's friend, or April's friend. This is how I had felt my whole life: invisible.

Triggers

In 1995, I was diagnosed with PTSD. My symptoms of extreme shyness, being withdrawn to the point of self-isolation, and the feeling of being unworthy of love all made sense. I started to identify things that trigger me.

Trauma can be triggered by all forms of sensory input, including movies, sound, and even smell. They can be as simple as not liking dark water. Well, don't let your four-year-old watch Jaws. It ruined my ocean experience.

My little sister doesn't like clowns because her mom took her to see Poltergeist when she was three years old. My big brother James instigated a fight between me and a heavy-set five-year-old girl when I was five years old, who lived next door. I was a tiny thing, and I rarely spoke around strangers, so James' big mouth convinced that girl to sit on me. She plopped her fat self on my back, and I could not breathe.

Struggling to get air into my lungs, I began to panic. It felt like the world started to grow dark. I reached out to James for help. It felt like slow motion. It must have been the terror in my eyes because he made her get off me. Once I was able to breathe, I broke out in tears, partly because I felt betrayed by James and partly because I did not know what I had just experienced. A good reason that I do not like to be sat on—just kidding. It was a funny story to tell later, though.

The most significant triggers for me come from the dark depths of my subconscious. They come from deep inside of me and can pop up at a moment's notice. It can happen in a crowd or with only a few people around. Sometimes it can even happen when I'm alone, because I'm an overthinker.

If a person grabs my shoulder, even gently, my whole body will pull away from them. A person can reach out, lay a finger on my back, and I will startle. Once during prep for surgery, after receiving Versed (a benzodiazepine medication used before surgical anesthesia) to calm my nerves and put me to sleep, the scrub tech pulled up my gown to place a warm blanket on my legs, and I reached up and slapped her. These defense mechanisms are vital to ensure we are never hurt again.

Recently, I was driving to work in my car and had the horrible feeling that Albert was following me. I shook off the anxiety, knowing he can't hurt me, literally saying out loud to myself, "Girl, he is dead, chill out."

I remember I slept so deeply, as a child, that waking me up was nearly impossible. This is when bad things happen. Too many times, I woke up with my little pants taken off and an old monster fondling me.

The worst memory was of me waking up, unable to breathe. That man had laid his whole body on top of mine. His chest pressed into my face, trying to have intercourse with me; I was five years old. To this day, if I feel held down, I will bolt. I have many other triggers, but they are faint and controlled. These are the ones that are the worst for me, the ones that I am still learning to control.

As for my childhood, we were very poor. We didn't have enough of anything. I can get over the fact that we barely had clothes that fit. Most of the clothes I wore were hand-me-downs from my brothers. I can get over the days without food. Parents try, and sometimes they fail. I had to run to school every morning to get breakfast, and I knew that when I left school, there was no food at home.

Have you ever eaten macaroni and cheese made with just water because you had no milk or butter? If you are hungry enough, you will eat it. When the weekends came, we hung around outside praying someone's mom would invite us in to eat a sandwich with them, but most times we went to bed hungry. These were the times my mom was between men, and she could not afford to feed us.

Healing

As I healed and grew spiritually, I felt that my story needed to be told. One of my younger cousins had confided in me that a neighbor child had molested her when she was younger. I felt confident that this was a time when I needed to share my experience and explain to her that the shame was not hers to carry.

I gave a shortened rendition of the hell I had walked through as a child, not knowing that she was going to run back to her parents and tell them. Maybe I should have known, maybe I didn't care at the time. I thought I was helping her. I was met with opposition. I was met by being called a liar. I was met once again with someone saying that I was trying to get attention.

Seriously, not the attention I would ever want. I do not desire sympathy. At that moment, my Aunt Lois came to my rescue. She had to be brave enough to stand up for me, even if that meant she had to tell her story to prove I was right.

She did, she told my uncle that I was telling the truth. She told my cousin that I was telling the truth because the man who hurt me had also hurt her. I do not know what happened to THAT aunt—the one who cared for and loved me. Maybe it was her trauma that finally caused her mental health to disintegrate. I know it can take a mental toll on a person, especially when someone does not seek therapy.

I often face opposition from my mom's side of the family. Now I feel like an outsider; I wear the badge proudly. I do not want to be known as a part of that "surname" family. I love my cousins, but not some of the elder family members who are attached to it.

I tried to be a part of it when my kids were younger. I attended a family reunion, and I was anxious the whole time. I was afraid to let my kids out of my sight. I looked around and thought about that family secret that wasn't confined to just my grandpa. He had a lot of brothers, and I know that sickness had to have spread throughout the park where I was. I felt sick; I felt shame; I felt dirty. I never attended another reunion after that.

Safe

As someone who does not like being touched, unless it's my idea, I love hugs. They make me feel safe. My greatest feeling of love is when someone's arms are wrapped around me. Why does a hug prove so much that words cannot? People speak words without giving thought to their truth, but the action of a hug tells the person receiving the hug everything they need to know.

How long is the hug? Is it tight, loving, and full of compassion? Or is it a short one, with a pat on the back and then a quick pull away? If the physical reaction of someone catches me off guard, I will question the integrity of that reaction. Truth to me is safety. I will question someone's motives until I feel safe, because trust does not come easily to me. Trust is a big part of safety. To be trustworthy, one has to be truthful.

CHAPTER SEVEN

A Dull Diamond Beginning to Shine

Chris

The same friends from Moore High School who were involved in daily marijuana intake were with me at a football game one night. We were hanging around the outside of the Moore High School football stadium, like the losers that we were, smoking pot. Over the loudspeaker, we heard, "Number 43, Chris Long, touchdown." My guy friend jokingly said, "You'll never get a guy like that." Quiet and in my head, I didn't care. I did not know who the guy was, and he had no idea who I was. It was irrelevant.

Fast forward nine years, I had my three Chronister girls, my niece, and my best friend's two boys. Yes, I had six kids. I always had a slew of kids with me. It was a rainy day in April, and the kids were driving me crazy. I took them to the local McDonald's in Moore. It had the best PlayPlace, and those kids needed to exert some energy. It was full. I think every parent in Moore had the same idea. We sat outside the PlayPlace to eat. Once they were done eating, I shooed them into the PlayPlace and prayed for a seat.

Right at the bottom of the slide was a very small, yellow bench. It had a child's coat, a cell phone, and a set of keys on it. I scooted the coat over, shoved the seven drinks under the bench, and plopped my 108-pound self down. Moments later, a man appeared before me, and I looked up. My eyes met the most beautiful blue eyes I had ever seen. Before me was this muscular guy, his dark hair brushed back with wisps of blonde in it. All I could muster was, "Did I steal your seat?"

He told me to scoot over, and I was shocked. Cute guys never noticed me—only losers, only players. He introduced himself. It did not hit me right then, the relevance of his name. It would be years later before I realized it was, in fact, the same "Chris Long." He asked me on a date, and my answer was, "When?" Strange answer, I know, but I made it a point never to schedule dates when I had my Chronister girls. They always came first.

For the first time, I had a guy page me back the same day. Yes, we had pagers in the late 1990s and early 2000s, especially if you couldn't afford a cell phone. He asked me what I meant by "when." After explaining the whole situation with my girls, he repeatedly asked if they were my kids and if he could see me after work on Monday. We barely left each other's side from that day forward.

Before I met Chris, I looked for love. If I were to start dating, I would fall hard and fast. I would give it my all. Picture a girl, perched on her knees, holding her heart in her hands. She has a smile that lit up the room. Her heart is so big, and it is so full of love. Each time a man comes along who seems interested, she holds out her hands for him to take her heart. She showers him with attention, devotion, and fidelity.

The man never reaches back. Instead, he takes the goodness from her but never takes the heart. She is left holding her heart, an empty shell of herself. Her light is fading, and she is lowering her head in self-protection mode. He notices her attention has faded; she is no longer calling or wanting to spend time with him. Her love tank is empty. The only thing she has left to give is her heart. He still will not take it. Instead, he starts showering her with attention. Trying to get back the things that made him happy. She is no longer interested.

This is how I lived my life. Personally, I still have that heart in my hands. I will wait until God brings me the right man. The man who reads me and understands that I am a survivor, a warrior. I may have been broken, but now I am healed. I am worthy.

Children

I've dreamed of being a mom since I was a little girl. I would take my dolls and arrange them from smallest to biggest and have them "grow up." A month after being with Albert, I had started on birth control. I experienced the first cyst on my ovary. This was an excruciating pain. Seven months later, the pain returned. It was so bad; I could not stand up. I could not pee. I went straight to the ER. I was told I had an infection in my tubes and ovaries. I was given a shot of pain medication, a shot of antibiotics, and sent home on three different oral antibiotics.

This started my long journey with reproductive issues. When Marty and I tried to have kids, we spent a lot of money and time looking for an answer. At that time, I didn't know my tubes were scarred. The OB I went to for three years never gave me an answer. He held my hand and told me to keep trying. He gave me Clomid, an oral medication used for treating certain types of female infertility. This was not a good idea for a woman who already had issues with ovarian cysts.

At age twenty-four, a friend told me about Dr. Kallenberger. One visit and I had an answer: Polycystic Ovarian Syndrome (PCOS). Basically, your ovaries are confused, and instead of releasing an egg, they decide that they want to make a lot of eggs but never release them. Then you end up with various stages of cysts on your ovaries—painful cysts. Dr. Kallenberger was kind and said that there was hope. I could do in vitro fertilization (IVF). This was something that only rich people could afford back in the late '90s, and something that only rich people can afford today.

During the time of infertility, I had my Chronister girls. They held me together. I put them before everything. Every person I dated would tell me to get rid of them because they were not my children. My heart did not know the difference. Their mother had abandoned them; there was no way that I was going to do that as well.

They came to my house every other weekend, as they would have if they were going to their mother's house. Chris was the first person to accept the girls. So, I allowed him to stay in my life. They grew up to be beautiful ladies, and two of them are the best mommies. We kept in touch, but when they started having kids, I backed away so I would not confuse their babies.

My Kids and Married Life

Max is pure joy. Born the size of a toddler at nine pounds and twenty-one and a half inches long, I labored for twenty-four hours and pushed for over one and a half hours with an empty epidural syringe.

I remember screaming for what seemed like eternity, waiting for the anesthesiologist to dose me through my epidural catheter so I could be taken back for an emergency C-section. Max's large head was wedged in my pelvic bones to the point where he had to be pushed back up into the uterus by the nurse during the C-section because he was stuck in my bones.

He came out with the softest cry and the cutest bottom lip puckering. The first words out of the doctor's mouth were, "Look at them shoulders." He had a bruise on his head from being pushed into my pelvic bones. I thanked God for C-sections that day.

I held him once my body was sewn back together, and I was in recovery. This special little gift that I thought would never be possible, I was now holding in my arms. We struggled to breastfeed, and I struggled not having a female present to help. I gave up breastfeeding after a week.

Chris was good with him. This was his second son. I started my last semester of nursing school when Max was two weeks old. My body was swollen and tired. I look back now and wonder how I survived. I had trouble lying down because I couldn't breathe, because I had pulmonary edema. My feet felt like I had water balloons on them, and I was so swollen from cardiomyopathy. Not to mention, they discharged me with a hemoglobin of 7.6. Yes, that's right, I had hemorrhaged, and they let me go home.

How I passed that last semester with my body, mind, and hormones so jacked up was truly by the grace of God. My mother-in-law offered to take care of Max while I finished school. At school, my arms ached to hold Max. He was so beautiful and perfect and sweaty. I'd never met such a sweaty baby; He was born in January, four days before my twenty-eighth birthday.

I worried that he would call his Nana "Mommy." I felt like I had missed out on so much of his first year of life. Chris wasn't working, and I was on the night shift as a brand-new nurse. I needed off the night shift before our marriage tanked. I needed the marriage to work for Max's sake.

My supervisor was gracious enough to move me to the Baylor Plan. This was where you worked for thirty-six hours on the weekend and got paid for forty hours. I worked twelve hours on Friday, sixteen hours on Saturday, and eight hours on Sunday. I wanted to raise Max in church; therefore, I worked the evening shift on Sunday. There were many times when I would sleep in church because I was so tired.

This change, coupled with Chris finding a job, worked. For over a year or two, we had the best marriage. I wanted another child; Chris did not, but agreed for my sake. We tried for over a year. We did all kinds of testing. Finally, one day at church I decided that God was the only way. I made my way down to the front of the church with my eyes closed, silently praying for another child.

I had a crick in my neck from sleeping wrong. I heard my father-in-law's voice approaching me. He was anointing people with oil and praying over those who were waiting. He placed the oil on my forehead, and it was like an electric shock flowed from my head to my neck, and the pain in my neck from the crick was gone. He had no idea what my request was before the Lord, yet he prayed fervently for me.

A month later, I showed Chris the positive pregnancy test. I wanted a VBAC (vaginal birth after cesarean) because I was convinced that I somehow failed the last birthing experience. My OB-GYN entertained the idea until my first ultrasound. Why did I grow such huge babies? It was another boy, and he was bigger than the first. I gave up the hope of a vaginal delivery and opted for a scheduled C-section at thirty-eight weeks.

He was twelve days early, and he came out at nine pounds and three ounces and twenty and a half inches long. He was as beautiful as Max, but different. Max was born with red hair and big blue eyes. Cash had coal black hair and the biggest brown eyes I had ever seen. He was also darker-skinned, as if the Native American heritage had been passed down to him strongly.

He seemed to breastfeed beautifully, with no issues and no struggles. On the day of discharge, at two days old, he had gone twelve hours without a wet diaper. The nurses said it was fine. This was back in the day when everyone got a free diaper bag with formula when they went home. This was our saving grace.

Early in the morning, the day after we arrived home, I woke up to a baby with sunken fontanelles. I immediately got a bottle and force-fed him. The next morning, during his first check-up, we discovered that he was tongue-tied and could not suck milk. He would have died of dehydration. I pumped for three weeks before I dried up. I felt depression creeping in slowly but fiercely. I failed again at breastfeeding.

At this time in our lives, we were living with my in-laws. We were waiting for our house to be finished being built. When Cash was two months old, we moved into our new home. One week later, we received a call from Chris's first wife's ex-husband. This man had a daughter with Chris's ex-wife. That dad was contacted by the police to retrieve his daughter from Chris' ex-wife's house. Chris needed to pick up his son, or CPS would take him. Chris rushed to get his son, whose mother had attempted suicide while the children were in the house with her. We all knew she was mentally ill, and this was the icing on the cake.

There I was: depressed, a new baby, almost three years old, and a stepson who was just evicted from the life he knew. This is when Chris decides to check out. I would wake up and find my stepson staring out the window, waiting for his mom to come and get him, but she was not coming. She had lost custody in an emergency order and had lost the ability to visit her kids unsupervised. He was nine years old and had lived through more hell than we knew. That is his story to tell.

I carried myself the best that I could. I cried through my shifts at work as a nurse. Once, I had to leave work because Chris left my stepson to watch

Max and Cash, who were three years old and five months old. My work was tired of the weirdness that came along with me.

Chris made it difficult to have a good work ethic. When Cash was seven months old, after months of telling Chris that I needed help mentally, I could no longer get out of bed. Depression was heavy on my heart. He brought the boys to me one day while I was in bed, and I rolled in the opposite direction. When I was not working, I slept. Then, he finally agreed that I could get help.

I went to see a doctor who had never seen me before. She knew nothing of my past, only the present situation. I was diagnosed with severe postpartum depression. I was prescribed Zoloft and sent home. Slowly, life became bearable. I began to lose weight and regained some confidence.

When Cash was ten months old, Chris had decided that he did not want any more children. He wanted a vasectomy. I felt like God had promised me a daughter. I refused to help him find a doctor. So, he found one on his own. He scheduled the procedure and made me drive him to the appointment. Once we arrived at the office, I refused to go back into the room with him; I sat in the waiting room.

Moments later, the nurse peeked out into the waiting room and asked me to come back as Chris wanted me to be by his side. I began to cry instantly and cried all the way to the room. It was a cold room, and he sat on the exam table in a hospital gown with a blanket draped across his lap. The doctor walked in, clapped his hands, and stated, "So, we are not going to do this today." I thought, "Oh, I am going to get into trouble."

He looked at Chris and said, "Look what you are doing to your wife." The doctor then questioned why I signed the consent. He could probably tell that I had no voice in the relationship. He then stated that he wouldn't do the procedure until I called back and made the appointment. Chris got dressed, and we left.

That was a long, silent drive home. As we were nearing our house, Chris finally spoke, "You did that on purpose."

I piped in, "I did not, I had no idea you'd pick a doctor with ethics."

The next few months were horrible, and by Christmas, I didn't care whether our marriage survived. I had decided that he needed that vasectomy. I called the clinic and scheduled it. The doctor was out on vacation for three weeks and would not be back until the new year. I did not care. I was done with that life. His controlling behavior was too difficult.

Three weeks later, and of course, all was good. We reconciled. Then one day, while we were sitting in the home office, the phone rang. It was the vasectomy clinic, reminding Chris of his appointment the next day. He became so excited, and I hung my head.

I had forgotten that I had scheduled the appointment, as I had made it out of anger. I silently said in my head, "Well, Lord, if you tell me that I'm going to have a daughter, I know you will give me one with or without a vasectomy." The phone immediately rang—it was the clinic, and they had to cancel because their machine had just broken. I do not know why I was shocked. God is that good.

Chris was devastated until I told him what I had said to God in my head. He looked at me and realized it wasn't me stopping this from happening. He decided that he would hold out on the procedure and give me until I was thirty-five years old to have another baby. Then he would have to get one, as we would be getting older. At that time, I was thirty-two years old.

I had a dear friend who desired pregnancy and had been trying to conceive for years. After multiple miscarriages, she was hopeless. I convinced her to see my father-in-law. She had said that she was not religious but was willing to try anything. We drove over to his house together. She sat down, and my father-in-law and I prayed for her while he anointed her with oil.

Can you guess what happened? Yes, I ended up pregnant a month later, but so did she with twins. Funny thing, my pregnancy was twins too, but I lost one early on. I joke that God knew we only needed one Fallon.

My beautiful baby girl was born in November 2006. She had a rough start and spent a week in the NICU (Neonatal Intensive Care Unit). She had a mediastinal pneumothorax and an open PDA in her heart (an extra opening in the heart that closes soon after birth). For the first three days of her life, I kept asking what was going on. The only answer I was given was that she had trouble transitioning since she was a C-section birth.

One morning, I waddled into the NICU for hands-on time. It was around 4:00 a.m., and I finally caught a doctor in the unit. That was when I learned about the hole in her heart and in her lungs. My heart broke.

Waiting until the family was awake was stressful. I was scared, and hardly anything rattled me. I waited patiently until 7:00 a.m. and then called Chris. I told him what the doctor said and that if the hole in her lung did not resolve, a chest tube would be placed.

At 11:00 a.m., it was hands-on time for Fallon. She had so many lines coming from her little body. Holding her was scary; I was afraid of pulling out her IV that was in her belly button or ripping the tape off her cheek that had on her CPAP, heart monitors, and warming probe sensor. It was intense for this momma.

During this visit, the secretary for the NICU called Fallon's pod and asked if the Garners could come in and visit. Shocked, I allowed them. They were my in-laws' friends from church, and here it was church time on a Sunday, and they were visiting Fallon. They had arrived to see my sweety while the church congregation prayed for her healing. I felt at peace.

The next morning, they gave Fallon her first bottle. Her heart PDA had closed. Insurance made me discharge from the hospital, as it was my fourth day. Reluctantly, I left. The following day, my mother-in-law's best friend

Jane drove me to the hospital to see Fallon and deliver her breastmilk. She was doing even better that day. Prayers were being answered.

On Thursday, I snuck out of the house at 6:00 a.m. and drove to the hospital by myself. This was wrong for several reasons: one being that I had just undergone major surgery a week prior and should not have been driving; two, there was a blizzard. I had to drive twenty-five mph all the way to the hospital. What normally would have taken twenty minutes took over an hour to get there. I could not imagine going for a day without seeing my daughter.

On this day, she only had a nasal cannula for oxygen, and she was feeding well by bottle. They informed me that she was stable enough to go home. I was by myself, and it was crazy weather outside, so I asked if she could stay another night and come back when I had help. The hospital agreed. The next day, we were able to take her home, well, first a stop by Jane's, as she seemed to hold my babies before my mother-in-law had a chance to. It is quite a good joke.

Life with this little girl has been such a blessing. Chris finally got his vasectomy, and I did not drive him that time. Pretty sure it wasn't as great as he thought it would be.

I had always thought that I was not that pretty, living in the shadow of much prettier girls. It wasn't until I looked at the face of my daughter that I realized every feature was beautiful. I knew at that moment—I was beautiful too. I was going to ensure that she lived the life I should have. She would be safe, protected, encouraged, loved, and happy.

During church in 2010, a dear friend told me that she hoped to be the kind of mother that I was. I asked her what she meant. She said that I always had a hand on my children. I was either running my fingers through their hair or scratching their backs. I was always loving, hugging, and kissing them. They never had to question if they were loved.

It made sense. You give away what you crave. My mom rarely kissed me, rarely hugged me. I only remember hearing "I love you" when she was sick and dying. When I was ten years old, I felt ill. I tried to lay my head on her shoulder, but she shook me off. I then placed my burning eye socket on her cold shoulder. This was when she realized that I had a fever. We were rarely tended to unless she thought it was warranted. Therefore, I made a priority that my children would never question their worth. They would know that their mother loved them.

My children also grew up picky about the foods that they would eat. Poor Max, he got my strange food aversions and couldn't handle the texture. Cash only ate cantaloupe, chicken nuggets, or grilled cheese sandwiches. Fallon would at least try new foods. My stepson would eat anything. I was the mom who cooked four different meals for my kids when they were little. I was not going to let my children go to bed knowing what a hurting, hungry belly felt like. I would do anything in my power to ensure my kids never know hunger.

Therapy, Again

Therapy is a strange thing. Sometimes you plan on it, and sometimes you are thrust into it. My second round of therapy was orchestrated by an intense desire to stand up for myself. I married Max's dad when he was five months old. I dreamt of a fairy tale life, complete with family dinners and family vacations. Many little girls dream of being a princess and being swept off their feet.

I've grown to realize princess stories are not real. It's never a fairytale ending. That grief that Cinderella feels while she is slaving away, tending to her stepmom and stepsisters, is reality most of the time.

After almost ten years together and the addition of two more kids, I left Chris, my third husband. He was a typical narcissist. However, I had never heard of this before my second therapy session. It had been fifteen years since I had been to therapy. I had healed my broken sexuality, and becoming a nurse helped me get over my shyness, but the vulnerable, people pleaser in me kept sticking around, letting everyone use her as a doormat. I always compromised to keep the peace.

Gordon Taylor was his name. He was older and so wise. Such an intelligent counselor. He had me take my first Myers-Briggs test. I always knew that I was an introvert; now it has been confirmed: I am an INFJ. One thing he taught me was the drama triangle, consisting of the roles of victim, rescuer, and persecutor. I was in this triangle with many people in my life. I had to find a way to break it. Breaking it meant it would hurt me or them.

My first break was with Chris. Since we had already separated and he was dead set on divorce, I let it happen. The second break was with my Aunt Lois—yes, the one from childhood, the one who told me about her trauma. That was hard, as she was one of the only people I trusted. She ended up being toxic. She would give gifts with strings attached. If you crossed her, she would tell everyone how you were using her.

Aunt Lois took more time. It took a year, and the first time I told her "No," it resulted in a snowball effect. She spread lies about me throughout the whole family. I was so hurt. I felt as though my relationship with my mom's side of the family was tainted. What hurt the most was that I thought they would not believe her because they knew who I was. My trust in her was gone!

After four and a half months, Chris and I reconciled, and I watched a narcissist break. Do not break a narcissist. Just leave. It's best for you and them. If you do break a narcissist, which is hard to do, you are just trading one form of hell for another.

Healing is not easy, and honestly, there is no endpoint. Each new issue triggers the other traumas to arise, and slowly, you learn new coping mechanisms to overcome each of them. Healing is also a personal choice. Each person is in control of their healing.

There are many times when depression can kick your butt, and you may not know how to overcome the suffocation of the darkness. I have been there. I have felt it. I felt it when my mom died. Even with most of our relationship being extremely toxic, I knew no other life. It felt normal to me.

After she died, and I had moved back to Oklahoma, I would sit at her grave for hours, talking to her grave or crying and fighting the urge to dig her up with my bare hands. I had the fear that she was somehow scared in the cold ground. These feelings only made me feel crazy. I later found out that many people share these same feelings, and I was not going crazy, as I thought I was at the time.

Success

My journey through college was a very long and hard road. After bombing out my first attempt in 1996, I had a student loan to pay back and a GPA of something close to 1.5. These were not going to help me enter a competitive field such as nursing. I paid off the student loan, spoke with the college, and found out that I could retake some of the classes for which I had incompletes or had failed.

I began my prerequisite journey, and after two years, I reached a point where I could apply to nursing school. I received my first letter of rejection. It was not as shocking as you would think. Getting an acceptance letter the first time was rare, unless you had a 4.0 GPA. I did not give up. I planned to take more prerequisites the following semester, which would enable me to achieve a better GPA and possibly one day pursue my bachelor's degree.

To my surprise, two weeks after my rejection letter, another letter arrived. It was a letter of acceptance. I was going to start nursing school in the fall of 2000. Ecstatic, I prepared for that coming semester.

I was also scared to death. The very first class was the fundamentals of nursing. I sat there thinking, "How does this pertain to the human body? Have I picked the wrong field to be in? Should I just quit? But how could I quit?"

I had spent the last two years killing myself to bring my GPA up to an acceptable level to ensure I could get into nursing school. I decided to stick it out. I struggled. It was not easy. I had no life! I could not see friends or family. It was either work, school, or clinicals. Having Philip in nursing school with me was a tremendous help. We would carpool to school together and sometimes we studied together.

We graduated in May 2002. We walked together, and we were pinned together. We studied for the National Council Licensure Examination (NCLEX) and we both passed. He went into the ICU, and I went into women's health; Two individuals with traumatic childhoods chose professions that help others.

In 2013, I decided that I wanted to go back to school to teach nursing students. While I attended the University of Central Oklahoma (UCO), a professor talked to me about alternatives to the teaching route. She talked me into getting my nurse practitioner license, as you could use your master's degree in nursing to teach, but it also gave you options to do more with your career. I graduated in December 2015 with my Bachelor of Science in Nursing degree from UCO.

In March of 2018, I took a giant leap and started my graduate program with Purdue Global University. Sometimes taking only one class at a time, it took me three and a half years to complete my Master of Science in Nursing program.

In September 2019, I had to start working two jobs to cover our household expenses. I was working two full-time jobs as a labor and delivery nurse while doing a graduate program in medicine. Challenging!

In 2020, I could only work one job, mainly because nursing was strange that year, and because I had clinicals. There were times when I did not have a day off. My oldest son, Max, was in high school. He was working and helping me pay the bills.

In December 2021, I was proud to see my name scroll across the graduation board from Purdue. I studied for my certification throughout the entire month of January. In February 2022, I successfully passed my certification to become a Certified Nurse Practitioner. Once I graduated and obtained my first NP (nurse practitioner) job, I went back to working two jobs to make ends meet again.

Nursing

My desire as a nurse was to work in labor and delivery. Partially because I loved babies, partially because my infertility issues made me in awe of the birthing process. After graduating from nursing school, I applied for a position in labor and delivery.

The Director of Nursing was an intelligent lady. She saw that I was not ready for that type of nursing. It takes balls to be that type of nurse. She persuaded me to join the Women's Center staff. I spent five and a half years taking care of precious women who were post-C-section, post-hysterectomy, post-mastectomy, or had a new cancer diagnosis. It was a great time to grow.

During my first week off orientation and on the night shift, I was given five fresh surgeries. The charge nurse took five post-C-section patients who were one to two days past delivery. For hours, I ran my tail off trying to get my patient's pain under control. By 4:00 a.m., after seeing the charge nurse in the break room watching TV, my quiet and shy self broke. I marched into the break room and said, "You will never do this to me again. You will make that assignment fair, or I will not accept it."

I went to nursing school with her brother. He was not like that; he was helpful. She quit several weeks later. I learned to speak up for myself and for my license. I spent six months on the night shift. For someone who loved sleeping, this was killing me. I also missed out on so much of Max's first year of life. My supervisor allowed me to do the Baylor Plan. This is where I remained for four more years until I had my Fallon and went part-time.

I say this to lead up to my time on labor and delivery. It was nothing like medical/surgical—it was scary as hell. Not only was it scary, but it was also emotionally draining. You had two lives in your hands. Sometimes, it goes smoothly; sometimes, you're in an emergency C-section where the cut time to delivery time is thirty-six seconds. Yes, it did happen. Dr. Driver is phenomenal.

The natural laborers, who really had no idea what they were getting into, were the most draining. If you tell a labor nurse not to allow you to get an epidural no matter what, please be prepared, and do not hate her later when she holds you to it. Especially when the ring of fire happens, or if you need to have stitches. The ring of fire is the burning pain when the baby is crowning during birth.

I delivered more babies than I can count without a doctor present. My calm, easy-going attitude often causes people to underestimate me. Although it is a great attribute during a scary delivery. Many times, I was told that my calmness helped keep the other staff calm. The patients would say it made them feel as though everything would be okay.

The quick decisions one needs to make during labor and delivery proved that it was not right for me. It led to nursing errors and nightmares. I grew exponentially in that field. I am grateful for the experience and the friends I made along the way.

Nurses eat their young. I took many young ones under my wing. I never fit in properly with the labor and delivery staff, either. Maybe, I wasn't bitchy enough. My personality did not fit in. Then one day, after a staff meeting, I heard God say so clearly that I was not where I was supposed to be. I cried. I was in graduate school, barely scraping by, with three kids at home and an unemployed husband, in 2020. I had been in labor and delivery for twelve years and had only taken care of women for the past 18 years.

I came home and mentioned to Chris what God had told me. I was spent from every item in my life, exhausting me; I cried again. A commercial for Shriner's Hospital came on the TV, and Chris told me to go work for them. Slighting him, I said there was not a Shriner's in Oklahoma. He always had a way of knowing things without knowing he knew them. His discernment was usually spot on.

He then mentioned a small hospital in Bethany, Oklahoma. At the time, it was the Children's Center of Bethany. I laughed; not the fun "HA HA" laugh, but a laugh directed at him for not knowing how nursing worked. Starting in a new facility meant starting on night shift. I was so tired. The thought of the night shift was appalling. To humor him, I opened my laptop and searched for this facility. There were many job openings, and to my surprise, there were day shift jobs available, so I applied.

Around six weeks later, I was offered a Zoom interview. Odd for me, but Covid made everything odd. The lovely nurse on the other end was kind and inviting. I had not previously experienced this level of kindness in the medical field. I was extended a job offer two weeks later. The pay was the same as what I was making as a PRN nurse.

It was a blessing, but it was different. I would now be in pediatrics, but not just any pediatric setting, complex care. Children with severe cerebral palsy. Children with tracheostomies. Children on ventilators. Children whose bodies were with us, but whose minds were not. Children whose minds were there, but their bodies did not work. So many new things to learn.

At or around month three, I found myself crying all the way home. I cried for three straight days. It was so overwhelming. After taking inventory of what was causing me distress, I realized it was the patient population I had cared for during my last shift. I had been placed with children in rehabilitation. These children were the ones who had new injuries, and watching their families going through so much stress was too much for my heart. I requested not to have rehab again and found my place with the long-term kids.

The chaplain of our facility, Dorothy, once asked me why I like working where I do. It was simple. I am a natural-born mom. I love children as if they were my own. At this job, I was a nurse and acted like a mom. I cleaned their faces and straightened their beds. I took pride in the fact that when they heard my voice, their heads would turn to see me coming, their smiles so big.

I did not always get to hear their words, but their voices were large. Their laughter is medicine to the soul. They knew their Mary. They loved me and I loved them. For that time, it was like I was their mom, and when I would leave at the end of my shift, I knew they were in good hands. This job is not a place to make money; this is a family.

Salvation

My journey may have started when I was seven, but it has been a continual growth. I started attending church by myself at the age of thirteen. Again, when I was a teenager, my friends and I attempted youth group—not to learn, but as a form of fun.

After I met Marty, I found a Methodist church in Norman to be married in. After our divorce, I was seeking a relationship with Jesus. I attended this church for several years with my Chronister girls. It wasn't until I met Chris that I found a church where I truly felt at home.

In 2000, when I met Chris, the girls and I began attending the Rock Assembly of God with him and his family. My girls loved the church. They looked forward to going. Eight months after Chris and I had started dating, he hurt me. Not physically, just emotionally. This is for another time, another story. It was December, and I had the option of ending this relationship and moving on or forgiving him. I was beside myself. I started seeking God more and more for answers. I needed him more than I needed a relationship with a man at that point.

On December 31, 2000, we were at church. There was an altar call. My eyes were closed. I felt like I had when I was seven, like a rope was pulling me to the altar. It was so intense; I could not ignore it. Not caring what anyone else thought, I darted out of that pew. I made my way quickly down to the area where I was supposed to go, eyes closed, raising my hands, laying my life at the altar; I gave my life to Christ.

It felt as though I was the only one standing there with God. Just He and I, alone, my soul conversing with Him. A washing of beautiful life and peace, overwhelming me. When the altar call was over and I opened my eyes, I was entirely surrounded by people. Those who answered the call, and others who were there to pray with them. I was in fact not alone up there, but my God was with me, one-on-one. He is my Father and I, His child.

Continued Healing

The craziness of healing is the fact that you only heal from what you know is trauma. Therefore, anytime any new stress or trauma comes along, you have to find a way to heal from that new experience as well. Not all past coping mechanisms work on the present trauma. We must continually evolve and always learn.

I spent a lot of my life letting people run over me. I thought that being nice was the right thing to do. Being nice is the right thing to do, but you have a right to say "No" as well. The part of being a good parent that I find the hardest is having to remain strong for everyone else when you are scared, stressed, tired, and exhausted. Learning to be strong, so your children can see you as an example of what it is like for a strong person to overcome when odds feel against them. That is hard, but very necessary.

My first time on a beach, seeing the ocean, was with Marty on our honeymoon. He took me to Seagrove Beach in Florida. We were staying at a cute house, right on the beach. I saw dolphins, a stingray, and a shark from our balcony. Showing up with the mixed emotions of what I had just committed myself to—scared that it would be like that first so-called marriage—I was numb.

Place a person with mental instability in front of an ocean wave and stand back and watch. I do not know what it is about the sound of the waves, but it unlocks the inner parts of your mind.

At first, I wanted to escape. I wanted to run away and not look back. These feelings that I had locked away were overwhelming, making me feel like I was going insane. Like I am drowning in all of the chaotic thoughts in my mind with each crashing wave on the seashore.

Fast forward twenty-nine years, as I sit on the beach, toes in the sand, listening to the ocean waves at 5:30 a.m., it is therapeutic. Unlocking the inner woven areas of my mind but also hushing all the fears. I finally feel as though I am thinking clearly. I am fifty years old now, not the scared twenty-one-year-old. For the very first time in my life, I am learning to love me. My goal is to love myself, not have a new degree, a new child, or a new relationship. I'm choosing me. The unfinished version, with rough edges and a beautiful heart.

Tommy, Crystal, James, Angela, Philip, and Mary

Philip, Bobby, and Mary

James, Philip, and Mary

Crystal, Mary and Angela

Mary, Phil (dad), and James

About the Author

Mary Long was a women's health nurse with eighteen years of experience before transitioning to complex care pediatrics. She has achieved her goal of becoming a Family Nurse Practitioner at Bethany Children's Health Center in Oklahoma. She is the biological mother to Max, Cash, and Fallon and a secondary mother to many children she has loved during her adulthood.

Mary's story is one of immense courage and resilience. It's not an easy tale to tell, but in her bravery to share it, we hope it will serve as a beacon of hope for those who are on their own journey of healing.